ERIC R. JUDGE, CFP®

OUT OF TOWN LANDLORD

LESSONS LEARNED

DURING THE

GREAT RECESSION

Palmetto Publishing Group
Charleston, SC

Out of Town Landlord
Copyright © 2019 by Eric R. Judge, CFP®

First Edition

Printed in the United States

ISBN-13: 978-1-64111-378-6
ISBN-10: 1-64111-378-2

ACKNOWLEDGEMENTS

To my wife, how did I get lucky enough to marry you? Thank you for your support and patience during our real estate journey. I could not have completed this book without your efforts and love.

To my son, thanks for your support and patience during our real estate searching trips. You are the best son in the world and your future will be full of great things. I look forward to seeing you make them happen.

TABLE OF CONTENTS

OUT OF TOWN INVESTMENT PROPERTY
(SEE APPENDIX FOR A FEW OTHERS)

INTRODUCTION

I have been investing in residential real estate since 2006 and I have accumulated a portfolio of properties in five states. It has been a fun adventure finding, purchasing, and leasing these properties, primarily during and right after the Great Recession from December 2007 to June 2009. Such an undertaking has not been without its risks. Prior to that time period, all of my real estate investing experience had been confined to my home state of Connecticut.

That made sense for me until two things happened. The first was that I was not successfully finding rental income properties that had positive cash flow or that provided adequate returns on my equity or amount of cash invested in my Connecticut properties. After all, one of the important concepts that I learned in the University of Connecticut's (UCONN) business school is opportunity cost. That is, you always should strive to invest your money in a venture where you obtain the highest possible return based upon the facts at that time. If you do not, then that opportunity has cost you the ability to apply that money elsewhere and earn a better potential return.

I had been looking for rental properties in desirable Hartford, Connecticut, suburbs with good school systems, and all of those properties were asking what I perceived to be a premium purchase price as compared to properties in other suburban towns. West Hartford and South Windsor were among the desirable towns for potential home owners and renters due to the great reputation of the school systems. That fact was known by the rental property owners which lead to their properties being in high demand. Consequently, they wanted a premium purchase price in order to sell their properties.

West Hartford, CT, is a suburban town with a mix of wealthy, high income earners, middle class, and working class people. It has a town center with a bustling mix of boutique shops and restaurants. The investment properties near the town center were really out of my reach. My financial calculations were showing that if I purchased one of these properties, I might not receive a positive net rental income for at least five years, and that was unacceptable to me. I know that the very successful California real estate investor, David Schumacher, made millions of dollars buying rental properties for which he initially had to put monthly contributions toward the negative cash flows the properties would experience for a number of years. In fact, he states that it took him seven years to achieve positive cash flow on his property purchase. [1] Those investments worked out well for him as the towns grew in demand and the housing prices in California appreciated nicely.

Due to the lack of attractive opportunities in June 2007, I decided not to make any further purchases until I could receive positive net rental income. After all, what is the point of owning a rental property if it is not generating any income?

I already knew the answer to that question. I had purchased my first two investment properties in my home market with the hope of receiving enough price appreciation alone to provide a nice return on my investment. Well, it took approximately six years to get positive cash flow on my first Connecticut based rental properties. My only consolation prior to that was that those properties were in highly desirable towns, and that the remainder of my real estate portfolio was able to support retaining those properties until the housing market improved.

The second reason for my interest in investing out of town happened in June 2009. One afternoon I received a telephone call from one of my mortgage brokers. What he shared would force me to re-evaluate the

1 P.12 Schumacher, Ph. D. David. *Buy and Hold: 7 Steps to a Real Estate Fortune*, (2007) U.S.A. published by David Schumacher, Ph. D.

principle that as a small landlord or real estate investor, one should only purchase rental investment properties within your local market.

The mortgage broker had called me to tell me about some REO or Real Estate Owned properties that his bank held. When I initially began to review the properties, I was overwhelmed because there were so many rental properties available due to foreclosures and underwater home values during the Great Recession.

The broker pointed me to a few areas with which he was familiar. I looked at a number of what is referred to as quads, four-plexes, or four-family investment properties in Killeen, TX, that were physically appealing and seemed to be priced relatively low. However, I knew that without being familiar with the area I did not know whether the properties were in good locations or whether the properties were priced competitively for the area. Accordingly, I was afraid to pull the trigger and buy a property without knowing the market.

It was time to get more information by doing market research.

First, I had to get comfortable with the prices for which the quads had been selling in Killeen, and for what amount each unit could rent. I began to study rents on the same streets as the properties I was interested in. I found they were priced such that the properties could positively cash flow.

It appeared as though the Great Recession was bearing a gift to me. As I began my investigative work, I found out that this area was definitely part of the pre-Great Recession housing market boom which had gone bust. The good news is that the area had a strong economic anchor in nearby Fort Hood as it is the third largest military base in the country[2].

Understandably, my first motive for being an out of town investor was to purchase a positively cash flowing property with good prospects for long-term capital or price appreciation. I had already played the do

---

2   April 13, 2016, website listing by *VeteranAid.org*. Fort Hood had a population of 217,003 while Fort Bragg and Fort Campbell had 238,646 and 234,914, respectively.

not worry about cash flow game, and I am still waiting to see whether I will see the long-term price appreciation that I had hoped for on that property.

I am fortunate that my three original rental property properties are located in strongly desired suburbs with very good school systems. When one of the tenants was moving to purchase a home, I was overwhelmed with prospective tenants and I rented the place within three days of posting its availability. Even the larger and so-called "professionally" managed properties do not have quicker average turnover rates than that. According to a multifamily executive website post, "Highlands Ranch, CO, based UDR…the average time it takes to move one tenant out and get the next one in currently sits at around fourteen days." [3]

Even better was that I got a second model tenant in the property. They take great care of the place and they pay the rent before the first of the month, The previous tenant had done the same thing. I was so lucky to get another great tenant in the same property and I hope they stay as long as the prior tenant did, which was four years.

My value to the reader of this book is my experience being an active real estate investor during the Great Recession, and seeking opportunities far outside of my local market and state. I have invested in five different states, and that geographical diversity has impressed upon me that all real estate truly is local.

That being the case, there are true benefits to operating in different markets. Some of those benefits are owning real estate in rapidly economically expanding geographic markets while other properties are in slower economically growing areas. I have now experienced real estate investing in both the up and down market real estate investing cycles.

Another value to the reader is my vast and insatiable investment knowledge. During my decades of working in financial services, I always focused on some aspect or sector of investing. My passion for

---

3 Isaacs, Lindsey and Mearns, Derek. "Keeping Turnover Costs Low" February11, 2013 *Multi Family Executive* magazine website posting.

investing was permanently burned and etched in my psyche as an undergraduate at UCONN with my first investment class, and it has never diminished. I consistently read such publications as *Institutional Investor* magazine, *REIT* magazine, *Barron's*, *The Wall Street Journal*, and many other financial publications in addition to reading many real estate investment books and general topic investment books.

I bring a pragmatic perspective honed from my good and bad experiences as a real estate investor balanced with financial theory. I also like to challenge conventional wisdom, which was the impetus of venturing into out of town real estate markets to purchase rental properties. I share my insights and knowledge so you can make a thoughtful attempt at investing in out of town real estate without too many of the lessons from the School of Hard Knocks. You can do without those lessons, as direct real estate investing requires that you actively participate. If you are not willing to put in the necessary involvement and oversight while still desiring to invest in real estate, then you might consider being an indirect real estate investor by purchasing a REIT index (a real estate investment trust) or another real estate security which allows you to passively invest through your brokerage account. Whether it is an appropriate investment for you needs to be determined by you or your financial advisor, depending upon your personal circumstances and your comfort level taking risks.

I am not recommending any investments as having better potential rates of return or success; however, I want to point out that contrary to what is in various other investment opportunities, a direct real estate investment is a bit like a contact sport. You do have to actively participate or you will be knocked around or out cold! If you behave like a real estate investor or landlady asleep at the rental property wheel, you may crash your personal cash investment as you neglect your rental property business.

The IRS has a different definition of actively participating in your rental property investments. As such, I strongly suggest that you carefully read the chapter "Real Estate Professionals and The IRS—Better to Think Twice," and then seek advice from a qualified tax professional before declaring yourself as such on your tax returns submitted to the IRS.

Lastly, I am a good landlord. Many of my past tenants remain in touch with me, send me pictures of their children, and have linked with me via Facebook. Although I treat my real estate dealings as business dealings, I am a firm, but always fair and ethical landlord.

My goal with this book is to add to the knowledge of those with some experience as a landlord or real estate investor. For those beginning, I truly recommend that you start as I did, by getting experience in your local real estate market first. Join a local real estate investment organization that does not sell you stuff and which also has a decent number of landlords with lots of experience.

In addition, I have included in the Appendix of this book a listing of some of my favorite real estate books. In my opinion, they are some of the best books written on various aspects of being a landlord or a direct real estate investor, based upon the plethora of real estate books that I have read.

My intention in writing this book is to provide the reader with things to consider if they decide that being an out of town landlord is an appropriate course for them and their personal circumstances. Such a decision should be based upon your financial resources, experience, and knowledge of being a landlord or real estate investor, your comfort with risk, your property management skills, and your ability to withstand any potential financial losses that could arise from taking such a course. Nothing in this book is intended to provide the reader with tax, legal, or financial advice. The reader is strongly recommended to seek legal, tax, and financial advice from professionals.

WHY OTHERS SAY
DON'T DO IT

I have read over thirty books on real estate investing. Many of those books do not offer the real estate investor any new or useful information. Most regurgitate the same ideas, or only cover how real estate investing will make you exceptionally wealthy. Granted, we all want to make as much money as possible investing. However, most real estate investors are not going to become super wealthy. I believe that one's real focus should be upon finding the most advantageous and optimal place to invest one's money and time.

Furthermore, the potential real estate investor should be aware that this investment is no different than any other investments, and it has associated risks and potential returns. They all should be weighed together from a knowledge standpoint and with a realistic assessment of the one's personal skill set and comfort with financial risk-taking.

Most of the books I've read are short on tangible strategies and systematic processes that the typical residential real estate investors can use, while the better written books authored by experienced real estate investors will tell you to invest in your own "farm area" or "home base." Although there is no agreed upon definition of home base, most would describe it as being within a one-hour to two-hour driving radius from your personal residence to your rental properties. Accordingly, they recommend that you only look for investment properties within an hour's drive of your home.

There are very good reasons to consider that advice. The first is that you will not be as familiar with the area outside of your real estate investing home base. If you are not as familiar with the area, you will not

1

know the best neighborhoods for an investment property to be located. You will also not know what is considered a reasonable price for an investment property in that area. Nor will you be familiar with the competitive rental rates. As a good Realtor® will tell you, real estate prices are derived from and most influenced by local factors and impacts.

Another reason given is that you will not be able to make repairs yourself, which can lower maintenance and repair costs for do-it-yourself landlords.

A common theme is that if you invest outside of your home base, you will need to hire a property manager, and that is not a path enthusiastically recommended. One assumption is that the property managers will not do as a good job as a real estate investor who manages his or her own rental properties. For the most part, I agree that a third party may not manage a rental property as well as the actual owner if they do not have the right incentives to do an excellent job. Furthermore, it is believed that small property management firms are incompetent, while large property management firms will neglect you...if they even take your business, since you are not economically worth their time based upon the revenue that you would provide to them as a small real estate investor.

There is also the thought that third party property managers should be avoided for an altogether different reason. However, most real estate professionals will not state it out loud. I provide more background and details on this topic in the chapter titled, "I think John Reed was Correct—Hiring Property Managers."

When I initially began investing outside of my home base I was astonished by how many repairs these investments were incurring, versus the properties I self-managed within my home base investing area. As it continued to occur, I became very suspicious. I launched a plan to send the tenants a customer satisfaction survey. In the survey I asked the typical questions, such as: Did they like the place? Did they think the property manager was responsive? How did they like the various repair work done? Unfortunately, no surveys were ever returned, even though I included a self-addressed envelope. Nevertheless, I did find a solution to drastically reduce the repairs at those properties. In the ensuing chapters, I will provide you with a strategy to mitigate that risk, and many others.

Finally, some will argue that you will eventually get tired of traveling more than one hour to an area outside of your home base.

As my primary motive for writing this book is to provide balanced and useful information to the reader, I present below a list of reasons *not* to invest outside of your home base. I truly believe that it is imperative to do comprehensive due diligence by analyzing all of the facts. In that vein, here is the list of reasons to not be an out of town real estate investor:

- You have better knowledge of your home base real estate market for renting, selling, and purchasing rental properties
- You can have more control by managing your property yourself rather than relying on others
- Your time and energy can be used much more efficiently without having to travel so far to show the property or to make repairs
- You may be able to build and maintain better relationships with the tradesman that you hire in your home base territory
- You will be able to build and maintain better relationships with tenants
- Lower repair costs if you are a Do It Yourself (DIY) landlord
- Lower travel costs, since you will not have to travel out of your home base market to visit rental properties

I could provide more detail on the points above for many more pages; however, I feel that plenty of other real estate books have expounded on those points already. My goal here is to make you aware of their main themes and to provide the opposing arguments. With those arguments, I provide you with more information so you might be better able to analyze more rental property opportunities fairly, and to make a final decision regarding which investment is appropriate for your circumstances.

REASONS TO INVEST OUT OF TOWN

Why should you pursue purchasing investment properties outside your home base? The primary reasons you should consider investing in rental properties further than one to two hours from you are as follows:

- Geographical diversification
- Potentially better returns on your personal capital
- Home prices in your investment market have appreciated rapidly and are now overpriced
- Potentially better or faster price appreciation
- Typically lower purchase prices
- Less competition with other real estate investors
- Better affordability for renters

Geographical Diversification

Different locations of the country have different opportunities in terms of employers, employment opportunities, educational options, income levels, cost of living expenses, and housing stock (including age and supply). Accordingly, you may be able to avail yourself of a rental property that has different economic drivers by going to a faraway town or a different state.

A basic principle of investing is that by diversifying or selecting different types of investments, you can reduce your investment risks or potential for investing loss. I believe that it only makes sense to apply this same principle to rental property investing.

At any given time, different regions of the country are experiencing different levels of economic growth in terms of population growth, job growth, wage growth, economic output of products and services, and new employers moving into an area. According to *Forbes Annual List of Fastest Growing Metro Areas* in a February 10, 2017, Forbes article by Samantha Sharf, the top ten fastest growing metropolitan areas were in the states of Florida, Washington, and Utah. The methodology of the screening focused upon population, employment, and homes values. The 2017 results are not an anomaly and support my point.

Better Returns on Personal Capital

Pursuing rental property investments outside your local market can diversify the rate of real estate portfolio value growth and rental income growth. In addition, it can mitigate the effects on your real estate portfolio profits of a local recession that causes lots of layoffs and negatively impacts the ability of your prospective renters to pay their rent.

The ultimate result of pursing a geographically dispersed rental real estate strategy is to have your poor performing rental properties offset by the stronger performers in a better performing geographical area. My experience bore this out by looking at the performance of my Atlanta investments versus Fayetteville, NC; Winston-Salem, NC; Killeen, TX; and Greater Hartford, CT. My Atlanta rental income grew 3.11% annually since 2009 while my Killeen, TX, properties rents would have grown only 1.75% (they were sold) and the North Carolina rents have grown 0.00%. That is not a typo. The Fayetteville and Winston-Salem rents have not gone up—not a one-hundredth of one percent, nothing. Compared with rent appreciation on two of my most attractive home base rental properties which grew 2.33%.

Lower Purchase Prices

One reason that I purchased two four-unit buildings, or quads, was that I could purchase them for $114,000 and $152,000, versus three family rentals in desired towns of my home base market for approximately

$300,000. At that price in my local market, the properties would not positively cash flow without purchasing the properties for 100% cash.

Less Real Estate Investor Competition

There are many real estate investors with too much competition in their home markets, and as such, they may want to explore real estate markets with fewer real estate investors. Although the heading for this subsection is "less competition," one must understand the factors that lead to *more* competition. Below I provide examples of one market with lots of competition. In addition, I discuss the impact of a more recent market player that may eventually dominate the prior province of mom and pop real estate investors. Even if it does not dominant the residential real estate market, it will have a profound influence on that market for years to come.

Denver, Colorado

I never experienced so much bidding competition as I encountered in Denver during the early phase of the Great Recession. To me, it appeared as though the Denver metropolitan area had an overabundance of experienced real estate investors, on a relative basis, compared with other markets in which I participated, and I believe it was the reason I could not win a single property bid.

Invasion of the Single Family Real Estate Investment Trusts

When I initially started on my out of town rental property purchasing ventures, the only competition in most markets was experienced local "mom and pop" real estate investors. By 2012, the larger and most attractive cities were besieged by the newly created Single Family Real Estate Investment Trusts (Single Family REITs). REITs are run by very sophisticated business and finance professionals, and many cater to large institutional organizations such as endowments, foundations, and pension funds. Traditionally, REITs invested in multifamily apartments, hotels, office buildings, malls, hospitals, senior housing, industrial buildings, and retail space.

REITs are mandated by IRS regulation to provide investors with ninety percent of its income via dividends in order to maintain the tax-exemption of income within the REIT. Those dividends are taxable to the REIT investor.

Residential family rental homes was not a market REIT managers viewed as one where they could operate efficiently enough to generate their expected level of profit. The Great Recession's massive inventory of homes got their attention, however, and may have forever changed the makeup of the buyers and the sellers of residential homes. On June 13, 2012, Bloomberg ran an article on its website which stated, "Investors are trying to spend at least $6.4 billion on single-family rentals, including from funds such as Colony Capital LLC, GTIS Partners, KKR & Co., Oaktree Capital Group LLC (OAK), Och-Ziff Capital Management Group LLC (OZM), and the Alaska Permanent Fund Corp. They want to take advantage of U.S. home prices for rentals, as the homeownership rate sits at the lowest level since 1997." The article went further to declare, "'Colony Capital, the private equity firm founded by Tom Barrack, is building an in-house staff to realize its plans to acquire $1.5 billion of rental homes by April of next year,' said Justin Chang, acting president of the firm's Colony American Homes unit. Colony, based in Scottsdale, Arizona, has acquired 1,200 homes and hired 125 people to buy and maintain properties in Arizona, California, and Nevada, with plans to add at least three other states this year, Chang said."[1]

When the Single-Family REITs initially began purchasing the homes, many said they would not stay as long-term real estate market participants. Well, they are here to stay! According to research from the Joint Center for Housing Studies of Harvard University, record demand growth spurred an influx of more than eight million new units of

---

1   Kenney, Allen. *REIT Magazine*, May/June 2017 edition. "REITS Flourishing in Single-Family Home Rental Segment".

rental housing stock in the United States in the decade between 2005 and 2015. Conversions of single-family houses from owner-occupied to rentals accounted for roughly 80 percent of the increase, as the single-family share of the total rental stock climbed from 34 percent to 40 percent in the ten-year period. "This growth is notable not only because it is so substantial, but also because institutional investors have taken a much more active role in this market than in the past," the Harvard researchers reported. "By creating large portfolios of homes across many markets, large-scale investors are testing the waters for a new model of owning and operating scattered-site properties that could expand the range of housing options available to renters."[2]

One should be aware that the professional investors managing large private multi-family real estate companies or multi-family REITs do not always master the data or listen to the local market experts. On the other hand, I might argue that they have an oversupply of money that they need to invest, and as such, they are willing to push or challenge local trends.

Why am I bringing up this discussion? I have seen these large professionally managed organizations spend millions of dollars on projects that end up not being filled to critical mass or they are built in areas that most locals view as less than desirable. It will be a few decades before the jury will truly be out or able to conclude that their bets to push what had been viewed locally as unpopular places to live are now the popular places for their target demographic.

The Single-Family REITs will have a big influence on the expectation of renters for desirable amenities in rental housing units. They will also compete with mom and pop real estate investors to purchase properties. In addition, if they decide in the future that they no longer want to be in the single-family rental property market and place large quantities of homes for sell in a local market, home prices in that local market will be negatively impacted. Accordingly, it is of the utmost importance

---

2 Ibid.

to assess the activity of Single-Family REITs in your out of town and home base markets going forward.

Faster Price Appreciation

Interestingly, Denver was also one of the first real estate markets to recover from the Great Recession[3]. The Corelogic Special Report *"Evaluating the Housing Market Since the Great Recession"* shows the Denver metropolitan area appreciating fifty-five percent from 2012 to 2017. Note also that housing prices decreased fourteen percent from the prerecession peak to the recession bottom. The residential real estate prices were as of the publication of that report up fifty-seven percent over the peak prerecession prices. That would have been a great market in which to have bought a rental property! Oh well. It's not like I didn't try a dozen times, to no avail.

Better affordability for renters

Some might be surprised that a real estate investor would care if the rent is affordable to potential renters, beyond a purely altruistic rationale for low income renters. Well, there is a business reason for paying attention to statistical measures that give you a sense of renters' ability to afford the median market-based rents in a particular geographical area. When this number becomes very high, your ability to find tenants who can pay your rents may be reduced, or the competition for those people becomes so intense that you have to lower rents. As many readers can also deduce from the aforementioned scenario, landlords with rent-burdened tenants may also end up with increased evictions and appearances in housing court. Increased evictions and additional court costs can have negative financial impacts on your rental property business.

---

3   P.11 Boese, Kater and Nothaft. *Corelogic,* February 2018 Special Report "Evaluating the Housing Market Since the Great Recession"

I know there will be those who argue they have a way to differentiate themselves enough that it will not impact them. That may or may not be true. My goal is to not to engage in that debate, but rather to provide the potential out of town landlord with some considerations with which to assist their decisions. After all, investing one's personal financial capital into real estate should be done with a long-term view, since you may involuntarily be committed to holding the property for many years.

What statistic should you use to measure such trends? Well, there are many. However, I like to use the median-rent to median-income, as it is direct and it is easily attainable. Financial lenders and others believe that most people should not spend more than thirty percent of their income on housing costs. According to the *Housing Affordability Burden for U.S. Cities* table listed on the *Governing States and Localities* website, New York City had 54.1% of all renters paying above thirty percent of their income, while Bellevue, WA, has 35.8% of renters paying over thirty percent of their incomes.[4] Furthermore, the median-rent-to-income in New York City is 32.2% while it is 23.9% in Bellevue. Both Akron, OH, and Charleston, SC, had median-rents to median-income at 34.7%, while the percentage of renters paying above thirty percent was 58.8% and 58.5%, respectively. You want to understand where your rent fits on the scale for that area while figuring out whether your proposed rents will attract higher income renters.

In order to be better able to complete the analysis needed for each of the reasons to invest in out of town rental properties, one will need to find the information that supports or refutes the reasons to do so. The next chapter provides you with some of the places where you can find such information.

---

4 Based upon information from "U.S. Census Bureau: 2010 – 2012 American Communities Survey."

WAYS TO INCREASE
GEOGRAPHICAL MARKET
AND PROPERTY KNOWLEDGE

G etting good information or access to information on towns and cities far away from your local area used to be a bigger deal prior to
the advent of the Internet. Obtaining the information you might have
needed on cities and towns in other states would have necessitated, at
minimum, a visit to a public library. Depending upon where your home
base was located, that may have required a trip to a library in a major
metropolis area. Many small town libraries may not have wanted to
spend money on such resources since they might not get sufficient use
to justify the expenditure. Nowadays, the Internet has many websites
which can improve your out of town market knowledge.

Wikipedia
I use Wikipedia as a good first step for many cities in which I am considering purchasing investment properties. I've found Wikipedia to be
very useful in providing an abundance of demographic statistical information. It provides good information on the map location of cities, the
population, the history, notable people who live there, educational institutions, climate, ethnic composition, income levels, spiritual organizations, and economic information. The two things I really pay attention
to are the median income levels and the employer information.

Nevertheless, you should keep in mind Wikipedia's potential weakness. The main weakness is that it can be updated or revised by anyone.

Obviously, that loose rule regarding who can contribute puts the information at risk for inaccuracies.

Local websites

Another way to get demographic information is to go to the homepage maintained by the city or town in which you are interested in potentially purchasing a rental property. Many city websites have lots of great information. For example, I went to the Fayetteville, NC, website before buying property there, and I found information on local attractions, events, higher education institutions, hospitals, economic development, employment, transportation, parks, and new resident information.

I find the local websites also give you a good idea of what the locals think are the nice features of their hometown, including the popular attractions, notable historical events, destinations, and other unique features.

Google Maps

Google maps is useful to take a birds-eye view or a street level view into the neighborhoods where a prospective property is located. I take note of where schools and major shopping areas are, in proximity to the location of the property I am considering for purchase.

Zillow

I use Zillow to identify the historical for-sale and final purchase prices of properties I am considering purchasing. If the specific property is not listed, try to identify an address for a similar property on the same street, to help you get a sense of the historical selling prices.

There are two other statistical information data points I found useful at Zillow. One is the historical property tax information, which is needed to calculate potential net cash flow, returns on equity, and ultimately to evaluate whether it is advantageous to bid upon a property based on such information.

The second statistical data point for which Zillow is a good source is potential rental prices for a particular property. I have found it to be fairly accurate. Sometimes you will also find the rents currently being asked by landlords or property managers on your targeted rental property's street or in the surrounding area. However, I use Craigslist as the final arbiter of what rental income a property could actually command from tenants, or should be earning from current tenants. That is where more and more rental property owners and property managers are showcasing properties to potential tenants.

Craigslist

Other properties on a street might provide a good benchmark of real estate values for a property being considered, since many times this information is not supplied by Zillow when a property is already listed for sale. Using Craigslist, you select the city in question to see a list of properties with similar market characteristics. When analyzing a potential property, you can get a sense of actual rents on a particular street by going to the Housing section. Select "Apts/Housing for Rent." In the search criteria, put how many bedrooms your target property has, and also put the street name on which it is located. It will show you properties on that street along with the rents that are currently being sought on that street. This will be your competition.

I find it useful to carefully assess the competition's amenities and features against my own properties to determine whether the rent I'm asking should be actually the same as, higher, or lower than competing rental properties. Studying the data over a week or two is even more useful, to get a feel for how quickly properties are being leased on the street you are considering. In fact, sometimes the posters to Craigslist have not deleted their older rental postings, and you will be able to estimate fairly precisely how long it is taking to find renters.

Trulia

Trulia provides much the same information as Zillow. I use Zillow mainly out of habit—back during the height of my out of town rental purchasing spree, Zillow was much more developed for my purposes.

Chapter Summary

Use the great geographical Internet tools available to increase your knowledge of out of town real estate markets.

- Wikipedia
- Local town and city websites
- Google Maps
- Zillow
- Trulia
- Craigslist

Now it is time to put on your big boy pants and have some fun exploring some of the considerations needed when purchasing out of town rental properties.

GOING SHOPPING - MAKING
MONEY STARTS HERE

When my mortgage broker notified me of all of the potential geographical areas with lots of homes for sale, it was initially overwhelming. Then my emotions quickly turned euphoric and my adrenalin began to rush like level five rapids. I realized this was an opportunity that I might not see again and I should take it.

I felt even more resolved in my thinking when Warren Buffet, one of the greatest stock investors and businessmen of our century, declared in a October 16, 2008, op ed, *"Buy American. I am."* He wrote, "A simple rule dictates my buying: Be fearful when others are greedy, and be greedy when others are fearful. And most certainly, fear is now widespread, gripping even seasoned investors."[5] Although he was referring to buying the stock of American companies, I took the liberty of applying that same rationale to buying American homes.

By October 2010, I had purchased ten rental properties and would make one more purchase in 2013. It was a four-unit rental property in Killeen, TX, that got the excitement going. That was the largest rental property I had purchased to date. It was built in 2002 and had approximately 3700 square feet. As they say, everything is big in Texas.

I purchased it for sixty-five percent of its prior market value and eighty-seven percent of its prior assessed value. The Killen area was full

---

5 P.A33 Buffet, Warren E. Op.Ed. "Buy American. I am." October 16, 2008: *New York Times, New York, NY*

of lots of newer quads. It was a clear example of the previous real estate building boom.

In 2010, I would purchase another quad in Copperas Cove, TX. I purchased that property at 60.90% of the peak real estate market value. This rental property had not been maintained well and needed lots of repairs. Even so, it had interest from other potential buyers, and I ended up in a multiple bidding situation. The real estate agent sent a multiple bid form to all parties to give their best and final offer. I raised my offer two percent and won the final bid.

Would you like a stove with that refrigerator?

Although the newly created Single-Family REIT operators with their billions of dollars in capital to purchase single family homes were extremely beneficial to price stabilization and removing the excess supply of homes from the residential real estate market, it was the mom & pop real estate investors like myself who were the initial heroes of stanching the depressed real estate market prices and excess inventory of residential homes. We were the trailblazers; other people were afraid or unable to purchase homes during the beginning stages of and immediately after the Great Recession in 2008 to 2010. The Single-Family REITS started purchasing in significant quantities somewhere between 2010 to 2011.

Real estate investors like me were the initial force that helped the real estate market purchase prices to stabilize. Most of the properties I purchased were missing refrigerators, stoves, and microwaves. I felt as though that type of purchase alone was going to pull the country out of the recession. We were not only taking the excess homes off the market, but by putting our capital into purchasing appliances that had been removed, and repairing burst pipes, putting in new carpeting, nicely painting properties, we were bringing many of the homes back to hospitable condition.

Flops

Not all of my shopping adventures went well. During the summer of 2009, I found a duplex in Schenectady, NY, online at a price that seemed attractive. It was an older property and I wanted to see it in person. Therefore, I convinced the family that we should take an impromptu trip—of which we are the masters. Schenectady is only a two hour car drive from our personal residence.

We decided to do a drive through the neighborhood to see what it looked like. After the initial viewing proved the area was safe to walk, we decided to get out of the car and look through the property's windows. We checked to see if the front door was locked, and amazingly it was not. We went inside and the place was a mess. It looked as though no one had done a repair or maintenance on anything in the place for fifty years. Everything seemed old and broken. After about five minutes of the inside tour we decided to leave. My son, eleven years old at the time, was at the head of the pack and when he went to turn the doorknob to leave, it fell off with the door closed and locked in place.

We were mortified; we were trapped! My son and I were left with no choice but to climb out the window. Once we were outside, thankfully the outer doorknob was still intact, and we opened the door for my wife. My son thought the entire episode was hilarious. My wife was not a happy camper since she had travelled two hours on a Saturday to see a dump, and to top it off, had almost been stranded inside a dilapidated building on a hot summer's day.

Later, in September 2009, my wife went on a weekend trip with her parents and her sister, Jeanie. By this time, I was obsessed with finding bargain properties. I found a three family rental property in Elmira, NY, priced at $40,000 and I could not believe it. I had no idea where Elmira was, so I looked it up on MapQuest and got directions. I was obviously late to embrace GPS in my car.

MapQuest showed it would take four hours and fifty-three minutes for the 298 mile drive. I asked my son if he minded going on a road trip with just him and me. He thought it would be fun, so off we went.

When we got there, we went to the property and waited for the Realtor with whom we had made an appointment to arrive. We waited ten minutes, and when he did not show up we called him on the cell phone. He said that he would be right there. He finally arrived twenty-five minutes late.

We followed the Realtor to the front door. He pulled a key out of the lockbox and put in the lock. He attempted to turn the key and it would not move. He continued to try it, shaking it to no end. Finally, he called the broker who had listed the property. The broker said he was at a wedding and could not leave. Accordingly, we had driven for almost five hours and would not even be able to see the three-family property. Needless to say, I was extremely frustrated. My son was a trooper and did not complain.

I figured that we should get something to eat for dinner and start our long journey home. At this time, I did not own a smart phone and so we just drove around town trying to find a restaurant. After about twenty minutes of searching, we came upon a nice-looking mom and pop diner. We ordered some basic Italian food that left much to be desired.

On the way home, I was cruising at about seventy miles per hour when out of the corner of my eyes, I saw something moving toward me. Before I could fully make it out, I realized that a family of deer decided to cross the highway. In a nanosecond I slammed on my brakes, just narrowly missing them. I was lucky that the brakes on my '9-3 Saab worked exceptionally well. Otherwise, that trip's ending would have been even worse than it had already been.

Property type considerations

My Great Recession rental property investments included condos, houses and four-plexes. Many experienced investors have a preference for the type of residential real estate which they believe is the most efficient, most profitable, or simply ideally suited for them. I encourage the reader to stick with the type with which they have the greatest comfort and knowledge. That is probably where you will be the most successful, based upon those factors.

However, I would also encourage the reader to at least do some quantitative and qualitative analysis on different types of residential real estate, based upon their availability in different geographical markets.

The long-held assumption that having more units in one location will be more profitable than a few single family homes in multiple locations, may not hold true everywhere and at all times.

My initial excitement and assumption that the best opportunity for the level of investment that I was going to make in Killeen, TX, would be by investing in a four-plex investment property would prove false. That market had lots of them, and many of them were less than fifteen years old. The entry prices were too attractive to pass up.

I was attracted to buying the two quads because I viewed them as "moving up" or becoming a more advanced real estate investor. I was definitely purchasing a rental property that would be more efficient to operate than four spread out single-family homes. However, my later experience and analysis would prove that I would have received more in net rent and price appreciation by having purchased two single-family or two duplexes in the Killeen real estate market.

What I learned was that prospective tenants in that target real estate market would pay a premium to be in a small single-family or a duplex rental property. I share this information in order to press upon the reader that you will really need to gather lots of information from many of the sources I cite in this chapter, as well as real estate professionals, in order to make prudent choices.

Returns on invested capital
You will need to calculate your projected return in capital as you analyze various potential rental properties in which to invest. Here are just a few needed calculations and financial considerations.

Monthly cash net rents before taxes
Monthly rent *multiplied* times a vacancy ratio *minus* monthly mortgage principal and interest payments *minus* monthly property and casualty insurance payments *minus* monthly tax escrow payment *minus* an estimate of monthly maintenance

Cash return on invested capital best before taxes

Net monthly rents *divided* by invested capital (total purchase cost including closing costs from HUD statement and rehabilitation or original repair costs prior to renting)

Present value of future cash flows compared with market value of property

Use an Excel spreadsheet or financial calculator to derive this very important measure of how much you should pay for a property.

Equity buildup from mortgage payments

Over time these need to be added to your invested capital ratio denominator

Potentially tax deferred income

In the earlier years of ownership, depreciation plus cash expenses may be large enough to shelter taxable rental income. One will want to discuss with your tax professional the implication of having taken the depreciation if the property is sold.

How many out of town markets

While you are having fun purchasing rental properties, there is one very important decision regarding how many out of town markets you want to own rental properties in. It is a personal decision for the reader to make. If I were able to jump into Marty McFly's DeLorean and travel back in time, I would have limited my own to one or two out of town markets.

Validated

It is noteworthy that during a live appearance on CNBC's Squawk Box, Warren Buffet told Becky Quick he'd buy up "a couple hundred thousand" single family homes if it were practical to do so.[6] My earlier real estate purchases had now been fully endorsed by the Oracle of Omaha.

Chapter Summary

- It is important to consider the types of rental properties in which you want to invest.
- Computing certain quantitative and qualitative analysis is imperative.
- The real estate investor needs to determine how many out of town markets in which to invest.

---

6 Crippen, Alex. Warren Buffett on *CNBC*: "I'd Buy Up A Couple Hundred Thousand Single-Family Homes If I Could." *CNBC website*. February 27, 2012

AUCTIONS - SOLD TO THE HIGHEST BIDDER

During July 2010, we came across a condo on a real estate website in Norwich, CT, which is an hour's drive from my home base. We were surprised at the super low asking pricing. When we inquired about viewing it, we were told that the seller was going to send it to an auction. Fannie Mae had contracted REDC to conduct the auctions. REDC auctions is now called auction.com.

On July 31, 2010, the entire family traveled to Boston, MA, in order to attend the auction for the property we'd seen online. The auction was held in a very large banquet room in a hotel. The room was buzzing with noise from the many conversations taking place between the hordes of people there to bid on properties that would be auctioned that day.

Well, the day had actually started with us bidding on a different property which was approximately fifty minutes away from our home base, located in western Massachusetts. My wife and I had previously called the Realtor to set up a walk-through, drove there, and completed our inspection of the place. We made a diligent list of the repairs, cleaning needed, and appliances to be bought. We calculated that for roughly a few thousand dollars of our savings and a few weekends of our time, we could have the property back up to a respectable appearance and rented. I estimated that if I could purchase it for no more than $75,000, it would have a positive cash flow and provide an immediate nice return on our original investment from the monthly net rent payments.

The bidding started around $50,000 and within two minutes, the bids had blown past my price and settled in around $87,000. Prior to the Great Recession the place had a market value of about $125,000. Luckily, we still were waiting to bid on the property that originally got us reviewing properties on the REDC website. It had been while we were researching the Norwich property that we found the one in western Massachusetts which we lost.

It was now time to bid on the Norwich property. The biding started at $22,000 and my wife had set her maximum price at $25,000. The auctioneer blew past that price with three of his auctioneer chants. There were two other people bidding up to that point. The auctioneer asked if someone would bid $26,300. "Do I hear $26,300? Going once!" I raised my hand. One of the other bidders raised his hand for $26,700. I raised my hand for $26,900, my wife looked at me in shock. This was actually not the property in which I was most interested. The auctioneer said, "Do I hear $27,000? Bidder, bidder, $27,000." I raised my hand again. It was down to just two of us bidding. The competitor raised his bid to $27,100. The auction said, "Do I hear $27,200, $27,200? Bidder, bidder, going once, going twice for $27—" Before he could finish saying $27,200, I had raised my hand.

The competitor would keep bidding until finally the auctioneer said, "Do I hear $27,500? $27,500 bidder, bidder." I decided this was my final and highest price. I raised my hand. The auctioneer muttered, "Bidder, bidder, do I hear $29,000? Do I hear $29,000? Do I hear $29,000?" I "tied" my hands under my legs as my wife looked at me with surprise that I was still in the running on the property that she had wanted but had quit bidding on after it went above her highest price.

Silence, silence, silence. Then, "Sold to the gentleman for $27,500!" The auctioneer's fee would add $5,000 to the price. We were not going home empty handed after all!

My twelve year old son was very patient during the four-hour round trip and for the two hours that we were actually at the auction.

On August 31, 2010, I called Fannie Mae's selling representative to find out the status of our contract on the condo unit. They told me the contract had been signed by Fannie Mae. I asked where the contract was and I was told that it had been sent to me via email. When I checked my email inbox, it was there. The property purchase closed on September 30, 2010. We spent the first two weeks of October painting, removing the old carpet, putting in new carpet, replacing the old kitchen faucet, replacing the kitchen flooring, replacing worn out outlets, and cleaning the place.

On October 13, 2010, I got home at 1:00am from working on the unit. I finished touching up the paint on the walls after the carpet installers left. In addition, I had quite a time trying to take off an approximately thirty-year-old faucet. After physically struggling for two hours trying to twist off the nuts on the metal water pipes, I had to go to Home Depot and purchase a metal cutting saw which finally did the job. The unit looked great. My wife did a great job of picking the contrasting neutral paint colors that accent the color of the carpet. We thought that all of our great work would make the place rent very quickly. The unit had exposed old brick and original exposed wood beams in the ceiling. The condo is located in an historic building sitting on a river with roaring rapids, which makes being there such a tranquil experience.

After a month of marketing, a tenant moved in on Friday, October 30, 2010. The projected annual return on our capital was 12.07% at that time. We still fondly reminisce about our entire experience at the auction in Boston. We were originally skeptical about auctions in general, and whether you would actually get a price that one would consider a bargain. The condo unit that we purchased for $32,500 had been valued at over approximately $60,000.

What I learned

What I learned quickly that day was, if there were more than a couple of people interested in the same property, the auctioneers would make sure the bids quickly exceeded the minimum reserve bid price. It was a beautiful thing to watch how they so artfully conducted this process. The rationale was that if they were not able to get the minimum reserve price, they reserved the right to put the property back on the for sale market.

In addition, if anyone interested in bidding on that property was determined to get it at all costs, before their heads were back in control of their emotions, they would bid way above their absolute highest price at which they should be buying such a property.

Do your homework prior to attending an auction by calculating your maximum bidding price and the resulting expected rate of return on investment. Then be disciplined enough to not exceed the highest price which meets the calculated required return on cash flow and long-term return on investment which would justify your bid price. Do not exceed it, no matter what.

Chapter Summary

- Winning properties at auctions is possible if there are only a few disciplined bidders with knowledge of current real estate prices.
- The bidding can be exciting. Accordingly, one must be disciplined in order to not bid above the desired bargain purchase price.

HOLDING TITLE TO PROPERTY

After you have had fun purchasing rental properties, you will want to consider how to hold title to those properties. Many real estate books spend a great deal of time on the topic of how to hold title to your rental property. Much attention is paid to land trusts, corporate structures, partnership structures, sole proprietorships, and limited liability companies (LLCs) as legal forms of ownership. I would suggest that a wise real estate investor would consult an attorney who specializes in real estate. You also want to make sure they are legally authorized to practice law in the real estate investor's state of residence and/or the state where you would like to own rental properties. Laws vary by state, and attorneys typically are licensed in only one or two states. Make sure that your attorney is licensed and knowledgeable regarding the laws that will pertain to you and your rental properties.

You might also consult an attorney who specializes in estate planning and real estate. Most important, it is not wise to count on generic information that may or may not be appropriate for your situation, and may even put your hard earned capital at risk. I tend to live a thrifty lifestyle, however, I find good advice valuable enough to spend the appropriate amount of my hard-earned money on seeking out professionals and not relying upon what my "smart," "sophisticated," neighbor, brother, sister, uncle, cousin, parent, or grandparent says to do. They may be smart, sophisticated, business savvy and moneywise. However, you should only seek advice from them in the areas in which they are professionals with the complete expertise to advise you. Furthermore, you should only seek advice from them if you are going to provide them with the complete details of your situation in order to allow them to provide you with an appropriate solution. Are you comfortable providing your family, friends, or neighbors with the most intimate details of your financial situation? If you aren't, it would be prudent to spend the money necessary to get appropriate information for your particular circumstances from a professional in that particular field.

Why all the discussion on holding title to the property?

Putting estate planning considerations aside, much of the discussion about how to hold title revolves around liability. Yes, we do live in a very litigious society where many people are looking to bring frivolous lawsuits and take the hard earned money that you and your family have sacrificed to invest.

Sole proprietorship

This structure is where your property is associated with your legal name. Accordingly, any potential lawsuits may seek damages against all of your assets and not just against the rental property from which the lawsuit is derived.

Rents collected, expenses incurred, profits, losses are reported to the IRS on your personal tax return.

Corporations

Setting up a C or an S corporation for your rental properties would create a separate legal entity from your other personal assets. The appropriate state filings would need to be completed.

All rents collected, expenses incurred, profits, and losses would be reported to the IRS as a corporate tax return.

Partnerships

If you are interested in investing with others who also want to make management decisions, then a *general partnership* legal structure might be considered. However, as general partners you will maintain full personal liability for the partnership and your partners' actions.

In order to limit your liability, one might consider forming *a limited partnership*. You would still need a general partner which could be a corporation. Nevertheless, as a limited partner, your liability would be limited to your own investment in the limited partnership.

The limited partnership would have relevant income and expense statements provided to all partners on an annual basis, which would in turn be reported on your appropriate tax returns.

Land trusts[7]

By creating a land trust and purchasing a property within a land trust legal structure from the beginning, you would be able to put a "veil" over the ownership. A land trust, like other trust structures, is controlled by a trust agreement. The trust agreement states who are the people designated to carry out the provisions of or manage the land trust. They are called trustees. A trustee is required to follow all provisions of the land trust. It also defines the beneficiaries of the land trust. A beneficiary is entitled to receive the income being derived from the rental property held by the trust.

The veil of ownership created by the land trust could be punctured by a court order telling the trustee they must disclose the name of the land trust beneficiary.

No special tax returns are necessary for land trusts.

LLCs

Putting rental property in a LLC has become one of the most popular ways to hold title for rental properties. This legal structure could make sense for many landlords, as it provides some limits on potential damages sought in lawsuits.

7 Shemin, Esq., Robert. *Secrets of a Millionaire Real Estate Investor.* New York City, NY: Dearborn 2000

The rationale is that you and the LLC are distinct entities. Creating these distinct entities may reduce the potential claims by not exposing all of your assets to potential lawsuits. For instance, if you only had one rental property under a LLC and there was a lawsuit brought against that property, then your other rental properties may not be subject to that lawsuit.

There are a few important considerations for the landlord and real estate investor considering a LLC legal structure. One is to have true separation of the LLC properties. You will need to have and use a checking account in the LLC name. You must not mix rental property assets with personal assets or assets not in the LLC's name.

You will also need to apply for a tax identification number, or TIN, associated with the LLC. This TIN can also help protect you against the overuse and overexpose of your Social Security Number to entities that do not need it and/or cannot protect it. Property management companies will need either your Social Security Number or a TIN to report to the IRS the rent revenues they collect on your behalf. Or if you have Section 8 tenants, the local Section 8 vendor will require your social security number or TIN.

After visiting the office of one of these entities to which you have given your social security number, you may feel there is very little protection against your social security number being stolen by an unscrupulous outsider, employee, or a hacker.

It is also important to have an operating agreement that defines how the LLC will operate, and the people legally authorized to operate it. The LLC owner must be disciplined to make sure those people are operating it strictly according to the operating agreement.

Transfer risks to the big boys and girls

Another consideration for litigation protection for landlords and landladies is to obtain liability insurance coverage. Why? Can you be 100% sure that the legal structures referenced above will be successful in preventing legal damages from being assessed against you and your assets? I am not suggesting that in all circumstance and all cases the various legal structures will not fully protect you from such lawsuits. However, a savvy attorney with the right resources and time may be able to pierce many of those structures and get to your wealth. Accordingly, it makes sense for landlords and real estate investors to consider transferring some of the risk to a good insurance company under the liability section of their property and casualty insurance coverage. Why not add an additional layer of defense since it probably concerns a decent percentage of your overall wealth.

This is where a good property and casualty insurance agent can provide value by insuring that your policy is appropriate for your rental property and you as a real estate investor. Claims brought against you by tenants and others due to your association with the insured rental property would have coverage if successful.

Equally, or even more important than having coverage for potential claims, is having an experienced team representing you. They'll have your interests in mind while attempting to prevent meritless claims from being successful, or to negotiate claims with merit to a lower amount. The insurance company with which you have liability insurance coverage has its interests perfectly aligned with yours—i.e. fighting lawsuits. They will be motivated to have their claims staff investigate each claim and, as necessary, will assign attorneys to defend claims against you. As the potential cost become larger, you can count on the insurance company to defend the claims vigorously. Accordingly, picking a highly rated insurance company that is financially strong is imperative.

The next chapter continues the discussion on how to reduce other risks in your rental property business. More specifically, the discussion centers around those risks associated with investing in out of town rental properties. In addition, I discuss some strategies for mitigating those risks.

Chapter Summary
How title to your rental property is held is an important consideration when trying to proactively avoid or mitigate liability claims.

There are many structures to consider:

- Sole proprietorship
- LLC
- Partnerships
- Corporate
- Land Trust

Consulting a qualified legal professional may be a wise and valuable move.

A real estate investor should have liability coverage under a property and casualty insurance policy, which is helpful when defending against litigation derived from your rental property ownership.

REDUCE BARRIERS
OR STAY HOME

As pointed out in the chapter "Why Others Say Don't Do It," there are a few obstacles to successfully selecting a property that is not close to your home base. The first is a lack of familiarity with the area and its real estate market. You will not know the ideal neighborhoods, the best offer prices at which to purchase property, and you may not be able to self-manage it. As a result, you may need to enlist the aid of a qualified real estate professional. Another obstacle is having your legal interests represented in your out of town locality. Furthermore, you will have to rely upon someone else to provide maintenance and repairs which, if the rental property was located in your home base, you would at least have the option to DIY if you so desired.

Finding a real estate professional
One way to find a real estate professional is to go online to look for real estate in a market in which you are interested in purchasing an investment property. Are there certain Realtors who have more listings than others of the type of property you are interested in? If so, you will want to call a few of those Realtors. I've found Realtor.com to be the most useful in finding Realtors to use as your local market scouts. The website shows agent names and agency affiliation for the listings you are viewing. A word of caution: when you are researching for properties on Zillow.com or Trulia.com, they show suggested real estate agents who are not the ones associated with the real estate listing which you are viewing.

A Realtor® might be of great assistance to you in finding properties in addition to also managing the property and tenants. There are some Realtors who are skilled and interested in doing both. There are also agents who are neither interested nor skilled. Therefore, you should also go to Craigslist, the Institute of Real Estate Management (IREM®), or Hot Pads to find agents who are active property managers in your targeted market.

You should select a few Realtors to interview. Here are some of the questions you should ask.

Interview questions
- How long have you been selling real estate?
- Are you an exclusive agent?
- What is your commission if I purchase through you? Who pays it?
- Will you also act as a property manager?
- How do you balance your commitments for selling real estate and your property management commitments?
- Could you recommend a few good property managers for me to hire?

Some things to listen for
- Is the agent professional?
- Can you tell whether they are having a good day or bad day?
- Do they sound friendly?
- If they have a property currently on a website for rent, do they know the facts about the unit they are trying to rent?
- Do they ask you any questions? An experienced Realtor® will try to prequalify you as a prospective client or property owner in order to not waste their time.

Based upon the responses you receive, you might want to enlist the help of two agents to maximize the number of potential properties you are shown.

Property manager

If the real estate agent is not also a property manager, or if you would prefer to hire a separate professional for each role, you might want to go to the website for IREM®. This organization is an "international force of 20,000 individuals united to advance the profession of real estate management. Through training, professional development, and collaboration, IREM® supports our members and others in the industry through every stage of their career."[8] Once you have selected a few property managers, call them and ask the questions below.

Interview questions

How long have you been managing rental properties?

How many rental properties do you manage? With thousands of rentals on their books, you may not receive great services unless they have lots of employees assisting them.

Do you use your own company or do you manage through a real estate broker?

How much do you charge? (for example, ten percent of gross rents for less than twenty units; five to six percent of gross rents for more than twenty units)

Do you have a handyman on your payroll or do you have long-term relationships with a few?

Do you use an attorney for your evictions? If not, how do you handle them?

How will you provide me with monthly account statements for my property/properties?

How will you provide me with my net monthly rent payments? (see the chapter "Collecting Rent—Electronic Payment Methods to Consider").

---

8 According to its website description *www.irem.org*

Find local legal representation

You will be making an investment of your hard-earned money, and you want to have as many people looking out for your best interests as possible. Real estate closings may seem very cookie cutter. Nevertheless, you will want a legal representative who does not treat it that way and who fulfills every necessary step on each transaction. I have purchased enough real estate to be very comfortable reading the documents and with the closing process. However, I hire my own legal representation to be at closings on my real estate purchases to ensure that the process goes as smoothly as possible and that someone has my interests exclusively in mind at closing.

That philosophy was solidified for me on the purchase of my current personal residence. We sold our first home almost twenty years ago and we were supposed to move into our new home on the same day. The moving company loaded all of our personal belongings into a big moving van and was en route to our new home. We'd left the first closing of the day on the home that we had sold and were on our way to the second closing of the day for our new home when we received a call on our newly-installed car phone (Yes that is correct. It was an installed in the vehicle. Just remember it was the late 1990s). The call was from our attorney, Patrick Lyle, who said that there was a problem with the closing on the new house. He proceeded to explain that the builder/seller had purchased a number of lots with liens put on them by the lender of the original real estate developer who had since gone bankrupt. As a result of this finding, the current builder did not legally own the land which he was trying to sell to us. My wife and I were shocked and the shock quickly moved to anger and frustration.

How could this builder's attorney have missed this? It was not just a problem on our future property, but on a number of lots that he had purchased in our future neighborhood. Naturally, the builder was livid with his attorney. Title searches are a basic step that all attorneys for real estate buyers should perform. This law firm had not only done a poor title search on one real estate sale, but on multiple transactions.

As a result of this huge mishap, our attorney negotiated for us to live in the property free of any charges until the liens could be removed and there could be a closing on our new home. Keep in mind the moving company was en route to meet us and unload our belongings into our new home. In addition, since we did not have the closing nor did we take title (think local taxes), or sign a mortgage loan (think no mortgage payment), we actually pocketed thousands of dollars which we would have spent on the mortgage and taxes for that month. That was a nice return on a few hundred dollars spent hiring a competent and disciplined attorney. It also took care of any potential future title problems for when we eventually sell the home.

One good resource to use to find an attorney who specializes in real estate law is the Martindale.com website. You can type in your targeted geographical area and check the box for real estate. The website has a peer review star rating system. Obviously, you should consider the attorneys with the most stars. I tested for a local area that I knew well, and found some of the attorneys I would consider hiring were at the end of the listing. Therefore, I suggest your review of attorneys should extend beyond the first page.

I know there are some very experienced real estate investors who have purchased and sold enough real estate that they have the words in each closing document memorized. However, most people have not had that much experience and, therefore, should seek a qualified legal professional.

In addition, you should be aware that if you set up your real estate business in anything other than your or your spouse's legal name, you may not be able to legally represent yourself in court. Accordingly, it would be prudent for you to have already selected counsel whom you can use when you need to evict tenants or to negotiate with tenants who might be suing you.

A lesson learned

I had to book five airline flights and at least two hotel stays in order to go to one of my out of town locations and evict a tenant for delinquent rent payment. This person knew how to work the system, and work the system she did. She even attempted to countersue me on the false basis that the heat was not working and that her young niece was exposed to health issues. For the record, there was never a niece authorized on the lease to live there, nor was the heating system not working. My total direct costs (airline tickets and hotel costs) and indirect costs (mostly opportunity costs of using vacation days) amounted to $6,125. It might have made much more financial sense to hire a local attorney instead of representing myself.

I believe that person avoided the property manager's screening process by having moved from another state and having it put on her credit report that her identity had been stolen. Seeing her work the system strengthened my belief that this was not her first rodeo, as they say. She navigated the housing court system like a pro. There were also a few steps taken that led me to believe she was possibly being coached by one of those free legal aid services.

Responsible tenant

You will sometimes be able to enter into an agreement with a tenant by adding a provision in the lease for them to assume certain responsibilities which might have otherwise been done by a tradesperson. Yes, you want to have it completely documented and not just committed to verbally. This will strengthen the agreement and provide clarification should there ever be any misunderstandings. In addition, people are pulled in so many directions in their personal and professional lives that details can easily be forgotten.

The lease provision should highlight clearly what is being negotiated. For example: "The Tenant agrees to cut the lawn every week from March through November or as long as the grass is still growing and reaches over four inches. The Tenant also agrees that the Owner has supplied a lawnmower to be used for the duration of this Lease Agreement. Furthermore, the Tenant agrees that the aforementioned lawnmower will remain with the Leased Property after they have moved out."

In order to have this be effective, the asking rent will need to be set below competing single family rents in your out of town market. The challenge here is to price it so the reduced rent is low enough to motive them to enter into such agreement, and to motivate them enough to actually honor the lease provision. In calculating the reduced rent amount, you must also weigh the rent reduction against a comparison with charging the full market rent and paying a professional lawn service to cut the lawn. You will obviously not want to rely upon the tenant to cut the lawn if the reduced rent amount would be equal to or higher than the charges from a professional lawn service. Accordingly, the reduced rent amount should be big enough to incentivize a tenant to move into your rental property, yet not be too close to the amount you would pay to have the services provided by a lawn professional.

We were lucky enough to have entered into such an arrangement with a tenant in one of our out of town properties. The tenants cut the lawn methodically for five years. The underlying critical key element to making such an arrangement work is that you are dealing with a responsible tenant.

How do you determine whether you are dealing with a human being who is responsible? Well, I have a few thoughts on what has worked for me.

You could have this as a discussion point during the lease renewal process and use it as a way to get them to stay if the tenant sees it as a way to lower their housing costs. What should you be looking for as evidence? What worked for me? Two things.

The first is looking for evidence of the tenants keeping their agreed upon commitments. This one is easy and obvious. Not only did they pay their rent every month, but when did they pay it? Well, in the case where we had the tenant cutting the lawn, they sometimes paid their rent before the first of the month.

This could also be applied to other things like removing snow or other things you would normally do. However, I might suggest limiting it to lawn cutting and snow removal. I had a DIY tenant once who would fix things and only ask that the rent be lowered commensurate with the costs of materials. However, this situation only worked because it was in my home base which allowed me to visit to check the workmanship. In addition, the person had been a home owner for many years prior and had honed his handyman skills.

The second consideration is to have someone assist you in monitoring whether the lawn is getting cut as agreed upon. In my case, it was a Realtor I would pay a fee to drive by and monitor things. You might consider other options.

Introduce yourself to neighbors

When you make your initial visit or a regular visit to your out of town property, introduce yourself to a few neighbors and give them your contact information to use if they ever need to get in touch. In addition, let them know that you may check in with them occasionally to ensure that the property is being properly maintained. With that comment, not only have you got a motivated set of additional eyes on your rental property, but you are building a good neighbor relationship.

Furthermore, you have created some good PR amongst the neighbors of your property if they talk amongst themselves by conveying the message that you care not only about your property, but about the neighborhood.

Like a good neighbor

I really think it is important to establish very early with the neighbors or the community that you are a real estate investor whose goals are aligned with other owner-occupied property owners. Sadly, there is a false perception that exist with some people that landlords or real estate investors are bloodsucking leeches who do not care about anyone else or anyone else's property. That false perception could not be further from the truth.

It is in the best interest of landlords and real estate investors to care about the neighborhood and community in which they purchase rental properties. Yes, we want an immediate return on our investments in the form of net monthly rental income or a positive net cash flow. But equally important is that we also get a long-term return on our hard-earned capital investment with good price appreciation on our rental properties.

Price appreciation will be influenced by broader, macro-economic factors such as employment growth, long term interest rates, and economic cycles. In addition, it will be influenced by micro-factors like the desirability of the location, its attractiveness, the quality of local schools, and crime rates. All property owners, including real estate investors and landlords, have a profound impact on the desirability and attractiveness of their neighborhoods. Trying to keep your property attractive with proper maintenance of the exterior and interior is a fundamental necessity for long-term price appreciation on that property. Accordingly, the interests of owners who occupy their homes and the investors who own rental properties in the same neighborhood are perfectly aligned.

Wise landlords and real estate investors know that keeping well-maintained properties in desirable neighborhoods makes it easier to attract good tenants who care about living in a nice community, as does having a landlord who cares about their property enough to maintain it properly by keeping it attractive and fixing things that break.

Chapter Summary

Hiring real estate professionals like Realtors and property managers to buy, sell, and manage your rental property may help you reduce barriers to out of town ownership.

Hiring a qualified and licensed attorney could be well worth the cost.

Having a responsible tenant may allow you to contract with them within the lease agreement for certain services.

Good relationships with your out of town neighbors has many benefits, including being an additional set of eyes on your property, and positive public relations to fight against negative perceptions of you being an out of town landlord.

HIRING PROPERTY MANAGERS - I THINK JOHN REED WAS CORRECT

When I purchased the four-plex building in Killeen, TX, I hired a property manager recommended by the Realtor I'd used to buy the property. That property seemed to have something break almost every week. I thought it was odd as the building was less than ten years old at the time. In addition, I compared it to my experience self-managing my rentals in Connecticut.

One day, I remembered something I had read in John Reed's book, *Best Practices for the Intelligent Real Estate Investor.* He mentioned that property managers sometimes steal, or create situations whereby they get kickbacks from tradespeople for work done[9]. They essentially have the repair and maintenance people either overcharge for the work or they create unnecessary work.

Dishonesty or poor management?

I felt this might be difficult to prove. I would ask the property manager lots of questions, and mentioned that in all of my time managing properties I had never experienced so many repairs. They said that these tenants were really hard on the place.

---

9 P.154-155 Reed, John T. *Best Practices for the Intelligent Real Estate investor.* Alamo, CA published by Joh T. Reed 2009

41

Within six months after this situation started, I received a gift in the mail. I had purchased two condominiums in Fayetteville, NC, and unlike the four-plex, these were built in 1985 and were starting to show their age with the mechanicals. A letter arrived from the condo association board stating that the A/C units and other mechanics were getting old and that owners should start to replace them. It also suggested it might be wise to purchase a home warranty policy, and mentioned two companies with whom others had a good experience.

The next day I called one of the suggested companies and set up the home warranty for future use. The policy covered electrical items, plumbing, appliances, central air conditioning units, and heating systems. I then called the property manager and provided them with the information to call the home warranty insurance company for any future repairs. It was like magic. The number of repairs on the four units went down drastically after I purchased the home warranty policy and instructed the property manager to use it. Was it a coincidence? I will never be able to tell you yes conclusively with 100% certainty. However, my gut and the information that John Reed provided both suggest otherwise.

Unfortunately, this was not my only experience being suspicious of too many repairs. It also happened with a property manager in Fayetteville, NC. Once again, the repairs magically went down after I purchased a home warranty policy on that property and provided the policy information to the property manager to use.

Most people do the right thing
I truly believe most people are honest, and it is just a few who are not. However, we need to run our rental properties like businesses and institute safeguards. I have found the home warranty policies to be a huge mitigation tool for excessive repairs when using a property manager. In addition, having a policy can assist in creating a more manageable monthly repair budget, knowing the monthly policy premium cost. My monthly policy premiums have averaged forty to fifty dollars for the states in which I use the home warranty policies. When you actually

make a claim, you pay a deductible of sixty-five to seventy-five dollars. I had originally investigated using the home warranty policy in Connecticut and decided against it as the monthly costs were approximately ninety dollars per month with a deductible of an equal amount. However, I am re-examining my assumptions and may purchase one for an out of town Connecticut property.

Under the home warranty insurance policies over the last eight years, I have received two new refrigerators, a new washing machine, two new central air conditioners units, a new heat pump, a new furnace, two hot water heaters and many electrical and plumbing repairs. I don't even need to do the math to conclude that I have made out extremely well by purchasing those policies, and gladly sing the praises of the insurance provider of my home warranty policies.

Not all of my experiences with property managers have been negative. In fact, many of them have been very positive. I had good experiences with property managers in Texas, Brandenburg, KY, and Fayetteville, NC.

Rosa and Felix, Realtors in Killen, introduced me to a good property manager in Copperas Cove. The plan was for him to be the property manager for the four-plex I had purchased. On January 27, 2010, I flew to Texas to meet with him. His name was Robert. He introduced me to his office staff, Dorothy, Simone, and Jessica. I was impressed with his operation, which included a residential sales division and a property management division. I guess I should have expected him to be on top of his operations since he was retired career military. His office was full of military awards and recognitions.

Key property management contract provisions

One of the important principles to have in mind in a property manager relationship is that your interests and the property manager's are properly aligned. You as a rental property owner want a tenant who takes care of your property, pays their rent on time, and feels they are treated fairly. There are many ways to structure the contract to achieve that goal. The usual way is to have the property manager receive a percentage of the rent. Typical fees range from ten percent of gross rents for less than twenty units and five to six percent for more than twenty units.

You might also consider a longevity bonus whereby you pay the property manger a bonus for tenants staying beyond three or five years.

Things to avoid or negotiate away

Do not accept provisions whereby the property manager will receive more money to find new tenants. I have always had difficulty with this provision, as it seems to incentivize a property manager to find questionable tenants or ones less likely to stay beyond one year. Thus, there will be a constant turnover of tenants, which will earn the property manager more money for every new tenant. However, the constant turnovers will result in less rent revenue for the property owner during the turnover periods. In addition, the property manager payments for a new tenant come off the top of the tenant's first month rent, not to mention the cost to refurbish the property between renters, all resulting in less money to the property owner.

Another provision to avoid is one whereby the property manager attempts to have exclusive rights to sell your rental property during your agreement period. My problem with this provision is that they may be a good property manager, but not a great real estate agent focused on selling rental properties. In my opinion, few are adept at being both a good property manager and adept at buying and selling real estate. The skill set of a good property manager and a good selling real estate agent only have a very small overlap of traits you would desire in each profession.

However, I do think it is fair to pay the property manager a commission for a property sale to a tenant they secured on your behalf if the tenant entered into a purchase agreement to purchase your rental property during the tenant's lease agreement period.

Keep in mind that property management agreements come in many varieties. In this section, I feel there is value in highlighting a few provisions which I think do not create a good owner-to-property-manager relationship. Your overarching criteria as to whether or not to include a provision in the property management contract should always be whether the provision properly aligns the property manager's interest with yours.

Thank you John T. Reed

I thank John Reed for being candid and sharing his inside experience and knowledge of being a property manager. I am grateful that an ethical person like him went into the profession. Otherwise, I would not have been aware of the few unscrupulous individuals who set out to receive money from kickbacks or charge for fake repairs.

Chapter Summary

Hiring a property manager is a very important process, and the out of town landlord must be totally engaged in the task. You will need to exercise due diligence to ensure that the property manager has all the necessary skills and is a good fit for you and your rental property.

Most people are honest. However, there may be a few unscrupulous property managers who need to be avoided.

A home warranty insurance policy can help you monitor repairs, and provide a way to keep your repair costs manageable. In addition, it can be a mechanism that can reduce the chance for kickbacks and fake repairs.

SELF-MANAGING YOUR RENTAL PROPERTY FAR FROM HOME BASE

While I have done it, I do not recommend it. At the end of the day, you will still need the assistance of a real estate professional. In addition, you will need a handyman at your disposal for repairs and maintenance. You will also need painters, carpet cleaners, and home cleaners.

I have successfully self-managed two out of town properties. In those cases, after finding the perfect Realtors (see the chapter "Reduce Barriers or Stay Home"), I paid them to find prospective tenants and to assist with getting a signed lease agreement from the tenant. I then worked with the tenant to make all repairs via a home warranty policy or using an online website to contract tradespeople directly.

Ability to hire professionals

Besides a Realtor® , another professional service that has made self-managing from afar workable is Home Advisor, previously known as Service Magic. I have used this website many times for my rental properties. Their services do not have a membership fee and the service received by each professional has turned out to be consistent with the ratings that I read before hiring them. I tried its better-known competitor first and I had a number of bad experiences with trade professionals that were highly rated on that website.

Home warranty insurance

A home warranty policy also assists you on the path of self-management from afar. As mentioned in a prior chapter, a home warranty policy covers electrical items, plumbing, appliances, central air conditioning units, and heating systems. You pay a monthly fee that may range from approximately forty to ninety dollars, depending upon the costs of trade services in your area. Provide the home warranty toll free number to the tenant to call when they need electrical, plumbing, or central air conditioning and heating repairs or maintenance.

Emotional quotient

One more consideration is, are you emotionally capable of self-management? Do you have great people skills? Do you have the free time available to respond to the calls from tenants or to call to secure the tradesmen for repairs and maintenance? Do you have sufficient property management knowledge to do a good job of self-managing your properties?

My wife has repeatedly told me that I should have become a landlord a decade sooner. My rebuttal has been that I was still not emotionally mature enough in my late twenties/early thirties to deal with a problem tenant. If someone had been hoarding in my real estate property, punched holes in my walls, dragged me to court just to prolong me from taking repossession of my property, urinated on my newly installed carpet so much that the smell could not be removed and we had to replace the carpeting and some floor boards (all of which has happened to me or my property as a real estate investor), the police would have had to be called in order to restrain me from causing bodily harm to the culprits! However, that would have been the wrong response, and my older self would have been forever disappointed by my display of low emotional intelligence (EQ) and lack of business acumen.

Everyone is different, as is the age at which you have emotionally evolved to be a fair, but firm landlord. It is imperative that you seriously consider whether you are yet at that stage. This self-assessment requires strong analysis of your interactions with others and of how diplomatic you can be. Strong relationship management skills are needed to be an effective landlady or landlord.

Semi-annual or annual property inspections

Another consideration is whether the property is cash-flowing enough for you to visit the property at least once a year. The visit should entail meeting with tenants and inspecting the property. This annual inspection visit should be included in the lease agreement so that the prospective tenant knows you will be hands on. In addition, it can save you some unnecessary tenant shenanigans as mentioned in the chapter "Do You Need to Hire Pearl the Landlord When Tenants Don't Pay."

Highest and best use of your personal time

Finally, you must also address the use of your time. This is not necessarily a purely quantitative calculation for everyone, but qualitative factors also need to be addressed. What are the true opportunity costs of spending more of your limited time on real estate investing? Will it infringe upon your personal relationships? Or is it a productive use of your time? There are many people who would simply be giving up a non-productive endeavor like watching television or aimlessly surfing the internet. It is these latter activities that I sacrifice for my real estate activities, as well as to write this book.

On the other hand, you may be in a profession where spending more hours growing your business by increasing the number of customers, increasing your knowledge of the business, working on visible and important projects for your employer, which will all increase your salary, increase your profile, get you promoted to a higher earning position, or increase the profitability of your business. If the results of these activities hold true for you, then you should estimate a fair hourly wage for doing them, and multiply that amount times the number of additional hours you contribute to your real estate endeavors. This resulting figure should be added to the expense column of managing your rental property. Then analyze what type of return on equity and net cash flow you would be receiving. That will determine whether self-managing your rental property from afar is truly a wise decision for you.

Chapter Summary

Self-managing rental properties from afar is difficult, and you may need to hire professionals or purchase a home warranty policy to make it work effectively and efficiently.

Serious consideration of your EQ is needed before becoming a landlord. This a tough business and diplomacy is required to be a success.

Assess what is the best use of your time and how the additional time devoted to being an out of town landlord can impact your career and your personal relationships.

GETTING THE PLACE
READY TO RENT - IT'S ALL
IN THE PACKAGING

After the closing of a rental property in Kentucky, I flew down over the weekend to meet with the property manager and to paint the place. My motivation was to save the money needed to hire tradespeople to do the work which would have totaled over $2,000. It could have worked out if there had not been so many other little undertakings that also needed to be done. I changed the door locks, replaced window screens, cleaned bathrooms and kitchens. I replaced missing light bulbs, replaced the trays on the stove, I spackled the multitude of small holes in the walls, and then painted as much as possible.

I'd had the property manager provide me with a list of items that needed to be done. However, some things had been missed and would have been noticed once they started working on the more obvious items on the list. Between the Realtor's walk-through list and the inspection report, I should have had a pretty thorough list of what needed to be completed prior to showing the place to prospective tenants.

If you have ever painted, there are a few things that slow you down. One is putting the painting tape on the walls where you do not want to paint. The second thing is spackling. There were lots of holes from nails and other mishaps that needed to be covered so the finish of the painted wall would look smooth and seamless.

When Sunday came it was time to get to the airport to fly back to Connecticut. I had only finished painting half the place with the first coat of paint. How frustrating it was that I was not able to complete the work over the weekend. I had just not been realistic with what was needed for completion, and what one person could complete in a forty-eight hour period. I asked the property manager to hire a painter to finish the job so we could get it painted and find a renter quickly.

Getting the placed rented as quickly as possible is the name of the game. So when I purchased the quad in Copperas Cove, TX, I made one of my conditions in the purchase agreement to be able to begin making repairs on the property prior to closing. The place just needed lots of small repairs. The maintenance needed on this rental property had obviously been neglected, as evidenced by the items noted in the inspection report. The biggest repair needed was to bring a firewall up to code.

It's all in the packaging

Have you ever received something that was nicely wrapped? Did you think that something really nice was inside because of the packaging? Did it make you feel good before you even knew what was inside? Did it increase your satisfaction once you opened the package? Most people like nice things, and with the influence of HGTV, it is an expectation for the renter and home purchaser alike to want to live in a home that by current trends is considered desirable.

"It's all in the packaging" starts with the very basic activity of thoroughly cleaning and sanitizing the place from top to bottom. You need to mop every floor, vacuum and deep clean all the carpets, clean the refrigerator and freezer of all food and food remnants, wipe down all counters, clean the oven of grease and burnt food (this is where you are very happy that self-cleaning ovens were invented), wipe down all light switches in the unit (oh yeah, over time you see dirty fingerprints), thoroughly clean the bathroom, and get rid of the scum in the tub, rings in the toilet, (oh yeah, someone stopped teaching people to clean the bathroom on a weekly basis), replace the caulking around the sink and bathtub, and either snake or use drain cleaner to clear slow drains resulting from hair and other buildup.

In order to assist with this process with current tenants, I provide tenants with a Move-Out Expectation Letter and explain if they do not adhere to it, they will be charged the cost of paying someone to clean the unit and return it to the way it was when they moved in.

Next, you have to paint the unit if it has not been done between a number of different tenants or it has been treated badly by the last tenant. I suggest a neutral color like beige or light grey in a flat finish throughout the whole rental. Then apply new white paint to the baseboard throughout. This will nicely accentuate the color palette. Remember, light and bright!

The efficiency achieved by having a favorite neutral color of paint in a flat finish is that once it is in place, you should just be able to touch up a rental property after a tenant vacates the place instead of having to paint the entire unit. Obviously, the assumption is that you have tenants that are imposing a normal level of wear and tear on the property. This process will allow you to save money, time, and to still present a nice-looking place to prospective tenants.

Rental advertisement

Part of your attractive packaging should be an eye-catching advertisement online. Earlier in the book I mentioned Craigslist, which I have used the most and had great success with. I have also used other rental property advertisement websites. Discuss this with your real estate professional, as there may be other sites favored by prospective tenants in your out of town market. If you are trying to manage it yourself from out of town (see the chapter "Self-Managing Your Rental Property from Afar"), you will need to do some research to figure out which website might be most advantageous for you.

Section 8[10] program details

Section 8, or as it is formally referred to by the U.S. Department of Housing and Urban Development (HUD), the Housing Choice Voucher Program, is the federal government's major program for assisting very low-income families, the elderly, and the disabled to afford decent, safe, and sanitary housing in the private market. The participant is free to choose any housing that meets the requirements of the program, and is not limited to units located in subsidized housing projects.

Housing Choice Vouchers are administered locally by public housing agencies (PHAs). The PHAs receive federal funds from HUD to administer the voucher program.

A family that is issued a housing voucher is responsible for finding a suitable housing unit of the family's choice where the owner agrees to rent under the program. This unit may include the family's present residence. Rental units must meet minimum standards of health and safety, as determined by the PHA.

A housing subsidy is paid to the landlord directly by the PHA on behalf of the participating family. The family then pays the difference between the actual rent charged by the landlord and the amount subsidized by the program. Under certain circumstances, if authorized by the PHA, a family may use its voucher to purchase a modest home.

Who is eligible?

Eligibility for a housing voucher is determined by the PHA based on the total annual gross income and family size and is limited to US citizens and specified categories of non-citizens who have eligible immigration status. In general, the family's income may not exceed fifty percent of the median income for the county or metropolitan area in which the family chooses to live. By law, a PHA must provide seventy-five percent of its voucher to applicants whose incomes do not exceed thirty percent of the area median income. Median income levels are published

---

10   As described by the U.S. Department of Housing and Urban Development's website.

by HUD and vary by location. The PHA serving your community can provide you with the income limits for your area and family size.

During the application process, the PHA will collect information on family income, assets, and family composition. The PHA will verify this information with other local agencies, your employer and bank, and will use the information to determine program eligibility and the amount of the housing assistance payment

If the PHA determines that your family is eligible, the PHA will put your name on a waiting list, unless it is able to assist you immediately. Once your name is reached on the waiting list, the PHA will contact you and issue to you a housing voucher.

Leasing to Section 8 tenants

I have heard some landlords say they do not accept Section 8 tenants. Landlords should know that it is illegal to treat potential Section 8 tenants any differently than prospective tenants who will not be using Section 8 vouchers for their rent payment. You need to apply the same screening process to all potential tenants. Furthermore, ignoring Section 8 tenants might be a mistake, as Section 8 voucher holders can be highly desired as tenants. They come with a very consistent and reliable stream of rental income. In addition, you will be contracting with a backer, HUD, which has the money and outstanding credit to make repairs when the tenants move out and there is minor damage.

Section 8 will require information about you, such as a social security number or TIN before you are approved to receive Section 8 voucher rent payments. The local Section 8 administrator will schedule an appointment to inspect the rental unit. They want to make sure it is up to safe and sanitary standards as defined by HUD. They want to ensure that the electricity, heating, and other systems are working. As an example of the kind of things they could request from you, after a Section 8 inspection of one of my units I was asked to replace a non-GFCI electrical outlet with a GFCI outlet in the kitchen.

For those who have never rented to Section 8 tenants, you should be aware of the different scenarios a prospective voucher holder may present. Some voucher holders qualify to have the full amount of their rent paid by the program while others are subsidized with less than 100% of their rent. Obviously, you are pretty much assured of receiving a 100% rent payment on a timely basis if the voucher holder qualifies to have HUD pay 100% of their rent.

I inherited my first holder of a Section 8 voucher on the purchase of a rental property. This family was responsible for paying twenty-five percent of the rent themselves. Receiving that twenty-five percent required extra work sometimes. However, what many owners find attractive about the program is that if you are in this scenario there is a contingency strategy to keep the Section 8 tenant responsible. The recourse is if you report their lack of compliance with any part of the lease, they could potential be removed from the voucher program. That threat alone is usually sufficient to gain compliance from the tenant when needed.

With Section 8, there is the potential for a portion of the rent to be at risk of not being received, but that scenario is no different than when you are dealing with any other tenant. What I have learned to be prepared for is the situation where a tenant starts out qualifying for a 100% voucher rent payment but subsequently has it reduced to a much lower amount. The typical reason for the change in payment status is that someone in the family has increased their income.

Another Section 8 process of which to be aware is that the tenant has to re-qualify for the program annually. In addition, your rental property and rent payments are also subject to approval on an annual basis. Accordingly, your rent payments from Section 8 can only be counted on for a single contract year. In fact, the rental amount that you seek to receive from the tenant and Section 8 in total is subject to criteria based upon the local market rents. This process also applies to all requests for rent increases.

My Section 8 experience

In my first Section 8 encounter, the tenant ended up causing some damage to the unit. I provided the list of repairs made, along with supporting documentation, to the local Section 8 administrator and I was 100% reimbursed. That was a big relief. I was concerned that I would get stuck in a bureaucratic mess and not be paid. To make my initial, unsubstantiated worries worse was that fact that the program does not provide security deposits. Instead, HUD guarantees that reasonable claims submitted with documentation will be reimbursed.

If you asked a room full of experienced real estate investors their feelings on having Section 8 tenants, the responses will run the gamut. My experiences are that I've had Section 8 tenants who were delightful and others who were dreadful. I even had one situation where it started out fine and ended poorly, due only to the poor decisions of an adult child who did not even live in the rental property with his family. To be fair and balanced, one should ask whether this is any different than dealing with tenants who do not participate in such a program. My response would be that this fits with the line from the movie *Forrest Gump*: "Life is like a box of chocolates, you never know what you're gonna get." Well, with all tenants, you initially will not know what kind of tenant you will get for their tenure in your rental property. You just have to try to meticulously maintain your tried-and-true process of interviews and background checks to try to screen out the potentially less desirable ones.

Chapter Summary

In general, people desire to have attractive things and to live in a home considered sought after by today's standards. HGTV has had a tremendous impact on people's current tastes and it has dramatically increased expectations of the living environment in which we aspire to live.

The Internet has many options for placing ads. You need to know the popular rental websites for your out of town market in order to be effective.

Section 8 tenants may be a reliable source for consistent rental payments.

You need to treat all prospective tenants with the same screening processes. Creating a tried and true standard screening checklist and always using it is important.

COLLECTING RENT - ELECTRONIC PAYMENT METHODS TO CONSIDER

The days of accepting checks is going the way of the dodo bird. Accepting checks not only forces you to wait to physically receive the check, but forces you to pray that the tenant actually has the money in their checking account so you can receive it in yours. Hopefully, you have not experienced writing checks against insufficient funds and having the deposit credit rescinded by your bank. If that happens, you incur penalty fees from your bank for the insufficient fund payments.

You can eliminate those risks by using an electronic payment method. As an out of town landlord, consider receiving your rent via one of the methods below.

A selling point to convert existing tenants to an electronic method is that it can make their banking information safer since the information printed on the check is at risk if it is lost in the mail. New tenants can be handled by making it a requirement in your lease.

Special bank account

You should establish a special bank account which is used solely for direct rent deposits by tenants. The money can then be transferred to another account that is used for expenses, etc. This will eliminate issues of receiving checks from bank accounts with non-sufficient funds. However, you still will be reliant on the tenant making timely rent deposits or transfers.

PayPal

You could also have tenants pay their rent via PayPal. This service solves the issue of receiving checks and it allows you to keep your banking information private. Your bank account is linked to your PayPal account, which you can then use for your rental property business. The disadvantage is that you incur a nominal fee on each deposit, unless you are family or friends with the person and you both have your bank accounts linked to PayPal.

Zelle

Zelle users can send money to other registered Zelle users. Users access the network within the websites and apps of Zelle-participating U.S. financial institutions and through the Zelle mobile app. There are over 100 participating financial institutions, including many of the largest banks, according to the Zelle website.

The Zelle network connects with existing bank accounts, so members do not need to fund a separate account to use the service. Only the recipient's email address or cellphone number is needed for a user to send money directly from their bank account to the recipient's bank account. Each email address or mobile phone number may only be actively enrolled at one financial institution in Zelle. To register at multiple banks, users need to provide a different email addresse or mobile phone number for each.

Payments made using Zelle cannot be canceled (unless an attempt was made to send a payment to someone who has not enrolled in the service). The Zelle service is intended for payments to those the payer already knows and trusts, and unlike PayPal, the service disclaims any responsibility for goods and services sold through the system.

This service also solves the issue of receiving checks and allows you to keep your banking information private. There is no cost for the service.

Have your own bank electronically pull the money

If your bank offers this service, you could register your tenant's bank account and have the rent payments withdrawn on a preselected date every month. This electronic method eliminates both the issue of accepting checks and the issue of relying on the tenant to make timely rent deposits.

A few electronic rent payment providers

Another alternative to accepting rent checks is to use an online rent payment provider. I have selected two below as examples only, since I have no personal experience with them. There are lots of new electronic payment providers offering various services at a cost, and it will take some time to ascertain which are the best among them and which to avoid.

- eRentPayment (https://www.erentpayment.com) allows for recurring and one-time rent payments. It costs $10/month.
- ClearNow (https://www.clearnow.com) is a rent collection service that directly deposits rent into your bank account. Costs are $14 month or $4 per semi-monthly payments.

ELECTRONIC PAYMENT METHODS	Checks Special Bank Account	Your Own Bank Electronically Pulls	eRent Payments	ClearNow
Cost:	$0.00	$14.95	$10.00	$14/$4
Risks:				
Exposed bank info	X	X		
payment timeliness	X		X	

Chapter Summary

Checks should be avoided if at all possible.

Use some form of electronic payment system instead of checks. Waiting for payment via the U.S. mail system and ensuring that funds backing that check are sufficient have gone the way of the dodo bird.

Continue to assess the effectiveness of electronic rent payment service providers.

THE IMPORTANCE OF
A NATIONAL INSURANCE
AGENT - NREIG

When I originally started purchasing rental properties, I would purchase the property insurance from a broker in each of the states
in which the rental properties were located. That meant dealing with
at least five property and casualty insurance agents in the beginning.
Then I discovered **ARPOLA** which had a marketing agreement with
the National Real Estate Insurance Group (**NREIG**). I saw NREIG's
website and decided to call them for information on the policies they
offer.

They had licenses in all states in which I was operating. Now I could
have one-stop shopping for all of my properties and only deal with this
one licensed insurance agency. That simplified my property insurance
process tremendously, and I have been extremely happy with their services, which include policy coverage statements, monthly billing, and
their crucial claim payment services.

Unfortunately, I can attest to their claims servicing abilities, as I
have had to make claims with them three times. All three times they
have provided excellent service. Two claims were fire claims and one
was for storm damage to a roof. All claims were paid without a hassle.

I have found them to be very competitively priced and their policies cater to the real estate investor. Furthermore, the policies they offer
come with an appropriate level of liability coverage as well as loss of
rental income coverage, and all of the other typical property coverages.

Loss of rental income

If you do not have this coverage on your rental property, *drop* this book right now, pick up your phone, and call your insurance agent immediately to add this coverage! This provision pays you the rent associated with property insured on the policy for a specified period of time for a covered claim. Based upon my experiences with a direct and an indirect fire, you should purchase one to two years of coverage if possible. My first fire claim was the result of a neighboring condo unit catching fire in the middle of the night. The two units directly next to it received the brunt of the damage. My unit was off to the side and below it with no direct damage. How could I make a claim, then, you ask?

That is a great question. After the fire, the town fire and health departments came and declared the asbestos in the building had been comprised, and as a result the entire building would have to be closed to all inhabitants until the asbestos was removed. I did not regain access to my unit and move a new tenant into my unit until a year later.

To top it all, about five months later, Bad Luck struck us again at a different property. This time a woman fell asleep smoking, and her unit caught fire. Guess what? She was also an oxygen tank user. She ran out of her bottom floor corner unit without her oxygen tank, and it blew up. I got a call from a fellow condo owner telling me the building was on fire. My wife and I rushed there to find the entire building ablaze. The flames moved violently up to and across the second floor. The firemen tried their best to put the fire out, but the fire damaged the entire building and it had to be razed.

How long did it take to rebuild? Two and a half years.

It is obvious with the second fire claim that my unit was a total loss and needed additional coverage than simply loss of rental income, which would primarily be covered under the master insurance policy of the condo association. However, the reader should note that my insurance claim with the first fire was for the loss of rental income even though my unit did not suffer damage. That claim was based upon a fire and my inability to continue collecting rent as a landlord.

Chapter Summary

Finding a national property and casualty agency which is licensed to sell insurance in all states can reduce the number of agents you need as an out of town landlord.

Coverage for loss of rent and a large amount of liability insurance are a must.

HIRING CONTRACTORS—ARE THE RATINGS RELIABLE? GET IT RIGHT THE FIRST TIME

For you DIY landlords, hiring a handyman or tradespeople will come as a difficult new task. However, it might be necessary in order to reduce traveling expenses or to get repairs done in a timely fashion, depending upon where your out of town rental properties are located in proximity to your home base. I found a service that has provided me with the confidence to hire tradespeople whom I will probably never meet, but with the knowledge that the final job will be done to my satisfaction.

That service provider is Home Advisors, originally named Service Magic. As I mentioned in the chapter "Self-Managing Your Rental Property from Afar," Home Advisor has been extremely helpful to me as an out of town landlord. The ratings of the tradespeople have held up to be true, unlike my experience with its competitor's service, which I will not name.

For the competitor's services I paid for a membership. I then picked a handyman service to repair a shower door, replacing caulking where the base of the shower door and the floor met. In addition, they were suppose to fix the screen to the sliding glass doors going out to the deck. The handyperson did sloppy work which rightly received complaints from my tenant, who sent me pictures of the unprofessional work. I figured I would get a second handyman from that same site to go and finish some of things the first one neglected to do. Once again, the resulting work was anything but good. What was disappointing was that both businesses had received very high ratings for their past work on the competitor's website.

Sometimes you don't get a second chance

I vowed to drop my membership and never to use the service again, which I haven't. The luckiest thing about the experience was that I found Home Advisor back in 2011. I have hired many different businesses using their website, and every job is done exceptionally well. It seems as though Home Advisor does a better job vetting vendors, based upon my experiences with both companies. I will not be giving the competitor another opportunity to negatively impact my rental property business again!

Chapter Summary

You should consider a reliable online website service in order to hire tradespeople.

It's always best to have things repaired promptly and accurately on the first visit.

SHOULD YOU HIRE PEARL WHEN TENANTS DON'T PAY RENT - PEARL THE LANDLADY

You may have seen the two-year-old landlord named Pearl in *"The landlord"* video that has been an Internet hit since 2007. The skit has her going to her rental property to collect rent from her tenant, played by the actor Will Ferrell, and includes her father, film director Adam McKay as the tenant's friend.

The skit plays out the story of a tenant being late on their rent and Pearl, is obviously not pleased with the situation as shown by her behavior. She launches profanities at the tenant and appears to have a drinking problem as played out by Will Ferrell's comments and her own words.

That is not behavior I personally endorse. I have stated earlier that I have honed a reputation as a fair, firm, and ethical landlord in my rental property dealings. I use the reference to the video to accentuate how we all might feel when the bad tenants try to take advantage of us and deprive us of making a return on the investment of our hard-earned capital.

Evictions

Having made my point about the wrong approach, let's explore what you should consider doing as an out of town landlord. You will obviously not have the convenience of knocking on your tenant's door. Although, that is not what one should do in the first place. It could be unsafe, and you need to follow the local legal and documented processes for evicting tenants or recouping past due rent from them.

You need to know the local laws on how to evict tenants. Seeking legal representation to do it might be wise. If your property is owned by a LLC or corporation, you may have to hire an attorney to represent the entity in court. However, you can self-represent if the property is held in your legal name, if you desire to do so.

In the chapter of this book titled "Reduce Barriers or Stay Home," I share my experience about having the right legal representation and how it can protect you and keep you from situations that can costs you lots of time and/or money. If you do not know the local laws and miss a step in that process, you will lose time in the eviction process by having to start all over, with the notice periods resetting from that time forward. Having to do that would only cause you unneeded stress and unnecessary aggravation.

If you are using a property manager, this should not be an issue. An experienced and good property manager will have a process in place, and people whom they use for evictions. In addition, you will have already vetted this issue with them if you follow my interview questions highlighted in that same chapter, "Reduce Barriers or Stay Home."

If you have hired neither a property manager nor local legal representation, you will need to spend time in advance to become familiar with the tenant eviction process and the process to collect past due rent payments from tenants in your out of town locale. You are going to have to master this process in order to avoid running afoul of the law and adding extra time to retake possession of your rental property. If you don't know the law, your bad tenants will know when you have made a mistake and they will attempt to capitalize on it.

Introduction to my version of Pearl
In Georgia, I stumbled upon my own "Pearl" eviction business. They solely focus on assisting landlords in filing the paperwork to either

recover back-rent or evict tenants, and to recover possession of their rental property.

During one of my visits to Georgia to evict a tenant, a nice woman named Fern stopped me, introduced herself, and explained her company's business model to me. I took her contact information and told her I might use them in the future.

The opportunity to use the services of Alpha Evictions and not travel to Georgia from Connecticut presented itself when a tenant, unbeknownst to me, had subleased the unit to his girlfriend's cousin. Apparently, this former tenant needed to leave town for an extended period and he did not want to break the lease. His idea was to enter into an agreement with his girlfriend's cousin and have the cousin pay the rent for the lease term. I will call her Alice. Well, Alice dutifully paid the rent on time for close to a year before I realized that Carl (not his real name) no longer was in the rental unit.

How I found out that something was amiss was when a rent deposit was not made. I attempted to contact Carl to ask him what the problem was. A woman answered his cell phone and told me she was Carl's girlfriend. I asked to speak with Carl and was told that he would not be able to speak with me. She proceeded to tell me that Carl was no longer living in the unit, but that her cousin was. She told me her cousin's name and gave me her cell phone number. I quickly called Alice and asked her how she came to live in my place. She told me about her agreement with Carl. I told her that she had not actually made a legal agreement with Carl because my lease specifically does not allow subleasing. Furthermore, the lease says that no one can stay in the unit longer than a month without my prior approval.

I offered to enter into a lease agreement with Alice, however I would need to approve her credit. I asked her for the all of the usual information needed from a prospective tenant. A few weeks went by and I received nothing. I called Alice and told her that she could not stay there without being approved, and without entering into a lease agreement with me. To my absolute surprise, she maintained that she already had a deal with Carl and she did not need one with me. Furthermore, she was going to stay there and not pay me a thing because my attempt to sign a lease with her was a renege on her deal with Carl.

I contacted Alpha Evictions and arranged to have them represent me. We submitted the paperwork in court to evict Carl and all others who resided in my unit. Alice was bold enough to respond to our legal complaint by stating, "Have been paying rent to Carl Smith/ was told and Can show owner is aware Did not want to Sign New Lease W/O Reviewing Ow(n)er wanted 1800 in addition to Rent." Can you believe that rebuttal? I wish I were making it up. However, that is exactly—excluding Carl's real name—what she stated, and the way she wrote it down, punctuation and all.

Alice was at least smart enough not to show up in court. Alpha Evictions was there on my behalf, and I regained my possession of the property in no time at all and at a reasonable cost.

Better to just pay them to leave?

Sometimes it is easier and less costly simply to pay the tenant to leave. I refer you back to the chapter titled "Reduce Barriers or Stay Home" under the "Legal Representation" section for a story that may provide you with more understanding for the reason behind that statement.

Chapter Summary

It is not wise to behave like Pearl the Landlady when interacting with your tenants.

Having a professional to assist with the eviction process and local tenant/landlord laws is even wiser.

RELATIONSHIP MANAGEMENT - CHIPS IN THE "GOODWILL JAR"

One of the fundamental underlying key principals to being a fair and ethical landlord is creating good, fair, and firm relationships with your tenants. As experienced landlords know, this is also helpful with tradesmen and real estate professionals. It is even more critical for the out of town landlord, as you may have to rely more on people closer to your rental property.

Good and clear communications
The basis of creating a good relationship will start by maintaining some frequency of communication. It will allow you to get to know them and them to get to know you.

Make and keep commitments
It will also entail always doing exactly what you said you would, and when you said you would do it. I know this sounds basic; however, you would be amazed at how many landlords do not do it. It will also mean immediately fixing all repairs that are needed. How do I know? Over the years, some tenants have conveyed how they've enjoyed dealing with me, and tell me the rotten things that prior landlords did, and the things they wish they had done.

Tokens of gratitude

Send thank you notes, holiday cards, and tins of cookies. I try to send a tin of cookies to all the property managers of my rentals during the holidays. I also send tenants holiday cards and gift cards.

I know someone out there is thinking you may want to be careful with the tenants, and not create the impression you are making so much money that they start demanding replacement of appliances, fixtures, carpeting, and repainting. This point is well taken, and I would suggest that good judgment is the key to not creating unnecessary issues with tenants.

On the other hand, I would argue that the landlords most concerned about this issue may actually need to invest in some upgrades to their rental property instead of those token gifts in the first place.

The result is priceless goodwill

This goodwill comes in handy if things go bad. When it does, you want to have a few good "chips" in the tenant's jar of trust. Otherwise, there might be subsequent lawsuits, anger taken out on your rental property, or baseless calls to the health department, etc.

What kind of events could lead to you needing to use those chips? I'll cover a few situations that happened to me.

A condo that I owned was flooded from the next door unit, which happened to be vacant. The tenant called, and I immediately called the local handyman with whom I'd had a good two-year-long relationship. He contacted someone to turn off the water. In the meantime, there was so much water in the unit that the tenant needed to temporarily move out.

That same poor tenant then experienced another water episode where he was flooded again. This time, the cause was that the root of a tree punctured a pipe, and the resulting flooding ruined the flooring of the entire first floor. Because of the goodwill chips that I had in the tenant's jar, the tenant stayed with me for four more years after the water incidents.

Chapter Summary

- Good, clear communication is vital to tenant relationships.
- Wise and good landlords fulfill their commitments to their tenants.
- Provide tenants with tokens of gratitude for being good tenants.
- All of the above actions create goodwill which is deposited in the "goodwill chips jar" with the tenant. You never know when you are going to need to use those chips.

CHECKLIST - DO NOT LEAVE YOUR HOME MARKET WITHOUT IT

I wish there had been a checklist for me to use when I first started on my out of town real estate investing adventure in 2009. I decided to include this checklist for the reader to use to reduce potential mistakes. It creates a repeatable process that you can modify as you see fit for your own rental property business and personal goals. The hope is that you will not feel like a prisoner to it, but rather, view it as a guide to some good standard processes. There are many things on it which novices and even experienced real estate investors might not think about unless they have been an out of town landlord.

In a January 4, 2010, *Time* magazine article, "*Atul Gawande: How to Make Doctors Better*" by Laura Fitzpatrick says Dr. Gawande advocated for doctors to use a check list in order to reduce mistakes. "When his team introduced a checklist, for one in eight hospitals in 2008, major surgery complications dropped thirty-six percent and deaths plunged forty-seven percent." In the article, Ms. Fitzpatrick was citing statistics from *The Checklist Manifesto*[11].

Obviously, real estate investing does not take on the specter of life or death like performing surgery does. However, you do want to do everything in your control to tip the odds in favor of having a well-run

---

11   Gawande, Atal. *The Checklist Manifesto: How to Get Things Right.* Metropolitan Books New York, NY 2009

and profitable real estate business. Even the world's greatest investor, Warren Buffet, uses an investment checklist[12].

Here is my checklist:

- Get prequalified or pre-approved for a mortgage if needed
- Set up LLC
- Interview and identify Realtors to represent you on property purchases
- Identify possible property managers
- Identify properties to bid on
- Find similarly sold properties to estimate a potential bid price
- Calculate your net cash flow and return on investment (ROI)
- Place a bid on property/properties with acceptable cash flow and ROI
- If bid is accepted, submit information to bank/mortgage company (skip this step with a cash deal)
- Contact local legal representation for closing
- Schedule home inspection
- Identify local handyman, electrician, plumber, and lawn service
- Request property insurance binder from property insurer
- Have attorney review closing documents
- Purchase title insurance
- Have real estate agent inspect property the morning of the closing to double-check for potential issues before closing
- Close on property
- Visit property, introduce yourself to tenants and neighbors
- Have locks changed
- Have extra key sent to you
- Schedule repairs for after closing
- Schedule painting

---

12 Hagstrom, Robert. *The Warren Buffett Way*, John Wiley & Sons Inc., New York, NY 1994

- Schedule carpet cleaning or floor buffing.
- Consider buying home warranty policy
- Have property manager list property for rent
- Have property manager complete tenant credit checks
- Contact local tax authorities with mailing address or P.O. Box (it is worth the price to not have everyone know your home address and to be able to keep your rental mail separate from your personal mail)
- Go to USPS.com and forward all mail from purchased rental property to P.O. Box
- Have rent automatically deducted from tenant's bank account and sent to you via an electronic payment provider

Chapter Summary

Using a checklist can make you more effective and efficient in your out of town rental property business.

Most important, a checklist can be helpful in mitigating the risk of making a mistake in your process.

REAL ESTATE
PROFESSIONALS
AND THE IRS

I am writing this section as a public service message. It applies to both home-based and out of town landlords alike. <u>You</u> should consult with your tax advisor before you attempt to try to use one of the passive activity loss exceptions for your rental properties. You really want an objective professional providing an opinion that you qualify for that exception. For many real estate investors, you will not be able to deduct your rental losses against wages. Although most landlords are actively engaged in their real estate businesses by being involved in the leasing, preparing the place for lease, doing repairs etc., the IRS will consider those activities passive. Losses on passive activities cannot reduce wage income.

Losses from passive activities may only be used to offset income from a passive activity. Passive losses that exceed the passive income for a given tax year is disallowed and should be carried forward to the next year, regardless of one's level of participation.

Real estate activities where one has materially participated would be considered active and would allow deductible losses. If one were able to meet the definition of a real estate professional, the losses would not be considered passive and they could potentially be fully deducted against income. Therein lies the temptation to be classified as a real estate professional for tax purposes. The new surcharge tax on net investment income may also make it tempting to try to claim status as a real estate professional in order to avoid having your rental estate income classified as investment income.

So, how does one qualify as a real estate professional? The IRS test starts with one of the following questions.

- Do the hours dedicated to the rental property business represent more than half of the total personal service hours the taxpayer performed during the year in question?
- Do those hours exceed 750?
- Does the taxpayer participate in non-real estate activities for work and is a W-2 employee? A yes answer to this question drastically complicates your ability to meet the definition of a real estate professional
- Does the taxpayer materially participate in all qualifying real estate activities?

With the questions above, I have drastically simplified the tax law language. Before declaring that you are a real estate professional for tax purposes, I strongly recommend you consult with a qualified tax professional who specializes or has lots of experience with the real estate taxes. I have heard from some impacted sources that attempting to use this exception is almost certain to get you audited.

I have also heard that you may be asked to provide proof of documentation of the time devoted to real estate activities in which you materially participated. I have included in the Appendix of this book an example of what that documentation might look like under 2010 Real Estate Activities. If you are audited for taking advantage of the real estate professional exemption to passive activity losses, you will need really good documentation of your qualifying activities.

Chapter Summary

If you think you're a real estate professional and decide to declare such on your tax return in order to avail yourself of more expense deductions, *consult a tax professional first* and *read this chapter ten more times!* This has been a public service announcement.

RISK TAKING - TRANSFER OR MITIGATE: WHICH RISK DO I TAKE?

Investing in real estate carries many risks. Not all risk can be totally eliminated. However, the savvy real estate investor's goal is to eliminate the ones that can be eliminated, and mitigate the severity or create a way to avoid those that cannot be eliminated.

The investor must have a very good screening process to select a tenant who will always pay their rent and pay it on time. However, no process can help a landlord avoid dealing with having to evict a tenant who has become too sick to work for three months and does not have economic safety nets to provide them with non-work-derived income. The screening process cannot protect an investor or landlord from the tenants who are laid off from work in a local market going through a severe economic recession.

Although the successful landlord has a great sense of other people's character, he cannot determine who will be the originally nice tenant who becomes a grudgeful one whom he has to evict, or a disgruntled tenant who decides to steal his appliances or paint the walls a deep purple out of spite.

A savvy real estate investor will have adequate property and casualty insurance on her rental properties. Nevertheless, she may not be able to prevent a tenant from smoking with their oxygen tank in the home, causing the unit to catch on fire. The real estate investor sadly watches as eighty percent of the building is damaged. The assessors declare that the entire building must be razed. Fast forward ahead, the town inspectors find asbestos which must be removed and slows down the rebuilding process. They also enforce new codes that raise the rebuild cost. The utility and water company declare that certain work is not up to code and extra work is needed. The twelve-unit building has not been rebuilt for over two years. Insurance covers only eighty percent of the rebuild costs and one year of lost rents. Yeah, I know I described my saga in a previous section. Please forgive me for restating it as it was very cathartic to get it out there again, and it is inexpensive mental therapy. Thank you for listening, and please send me your therapy session bill!

Risk taking comfort

Do you have financial risk-taking in your DNA? There are those amongst us who will quit their job to return to school full-time in the hopes that an advanced degree will produce a higher immediate and lifetime income. There are those who will quit their job to launch a new business venture. Some people would think nothing of quitting their well-paying job, selling their home, removing their kids from school, and going on a one-year trip around the world. How do you measure on this type of risk-taking meter?

A real estate investor, be she home based or out of town, needs to know their own threshold for financial pain. Would you be able to sleep at night if you took $100,000 (insert a dollar amount that is substantial for your financial resources) of your family's capital and invested it in a rental property which twenty years after the purchase provided your family with zero dollars back?

Risk transfer

One of the easiest and best ways to reduce or transfer risk is by purchasing property and casualty insurance on your rental properties. By purchasing the policy, the investor is transferring some of the risk while sharing in some of the potential financial losses from property damage and other risks associated with the rental property ownership.

Risk mitigation

Throughout this book, I have presented ideas and services to use in order to transfer, share in, or mitigate as many of the potential risks associated with being an out of town landlord as possible. As those of us who have lived long enough know, experiencing some of life's unexpected events is part of our life's journey. I must remind the readers that an out of town landlord's journey may provide them with many chapters for the book of their life's journey, or at least for good stories at cocktail parties.

That being said, by using some of the things presented earlier in the book, such as using Realtors and property managers, using attorneys, investing in economically-growing markets, purchasing title insurance, property insurance, and home warranty insurance, and using the ratings on Home Advisor to hire tradespeople and handymen, you may be able to reduce, eliminate, or transfer some of that risk.

Total risk elimination impossible

All investing comes with some form of risk, and that includes real estate investing. Some forms of investing carry higher potential risks of losing your investment. The correlated potential return should be relatively higher than those investment opportunities with low risks. Otherwise, a rational person should simply avoid such potential loss of their hard-earned personal capital and simplify their life by putting it in a FDIC insured bank savings account. It would only make sense to take an opportunity that can provide you with a higher rate of return of your investment than the savings account, for the same or lower level of risk.

In real estate, it is said that in order to receive the optimal investment return for a property, one must figure out the highest and best use of a property. I believe that as one is contemplating any investment of one's hard-earned money, one should give serious thought to what might provide the optimal return to them for a given level of risk. In my life's journey, I have learned that what might seem like little to no risk to one person could feel tremendously risky to another person. Each person must define their own level of comfort with the risks presented by the investment ventures which they seek out.

What one considers less risky at one point, may change in time

At a much earlier stage of my life, I was not emotionally prepared to deal with tenants not paying the rent owed to me, tenants damaging my property, or that the value of my investment may not appreciate as well as I originally estimated. It was through experiences and greater knowledge that my level of comfort with those risks increased. What is to be noted is that the potential risk of loss from those situations has not changed, however my comfort level with them did change. And my comfort level with those things might well change again in the future as my personal financial goals and my ability to manage my real estate portfolio changes. Savvy investors would agree that it is wise to continuously review one's original assumptions against one's changing personal circumstances. We know that life is not static, but forever changing.

The two four-plexes in Texas were the original properties that fueled my desire to be an out of town landlord. I have since sold them, because my comfort with the level of risk which came with their continued ownership and the future projected returns on my investment were no longer high enough to justify those risks. I have not regretted buying or selling the two four-plexes. We came out with our shirts intact. There was a time when I doubted that would be the case. It was a very bumpy ownership ride. I have never seen such high tenant turnover. Nevertheless, it was worth it, as I could never have gained the knowledge that I did without having experienced those things firsthand as an owner.

Risk avoidance

The simplest and most obvious way to avoid risks that cannot be eliminated is to not invest in that rental property, or to avoid the event which presents such a risk. For example, the risk that in spite of your great preparation prior to buying a property in a desirable neighborhood in an area which is economically growing, politically stable, and to which you have diligently applied savvy property management, you find yourself with a property that does not give a financial return on your investment.

Once that is the situation, the only way to truly avoid the risk of it getting worse might be to sell it.

Know and understand the risk that you are accepting

As I stated in the beginning of this book, my intent in writing it was to attempt to save the inexperienced out of town real estate investor from having such a steep learning curve on their lessons from being an out of town landlord. I have read lots of great real estate books, and none of them have provided information on how to manage out of town rental properties. In this book I have provided what I consider to be some important considerations for those interested in exploring investments outside of their home base real estate market.

These considerations should help mitigate some of the risk. Nevertheless, risk will remain. It is the responsibility of each real estate investor to know and fully understand what risks they are willing to accept from a financial, emotional, and a time commitment standpoint.

A fundamental investing principle is balancing potential risks with potential rewards. The expected return on your investment of personal capital must sufficiently compensate you for the expected risk you will be taking. The higher the expected risk, the higher the return should be, compared with potential alternative investments with lower expected risks. You have to establish your criteria for what makes sense for you. When an investment opportunity does not make sense or meet your minimum floor for expected potential return to investment, keep your powder dry, as the saying goes.

My main point here is that you need to have all of the available information from as many sources as possible to make prudent decisions. If you decide to go against the data, and your financial resources are substantial, well, it's your money. You have made a conscious decision to ignore the risks. Just be absolutely certain you knowingly and willingly accept the potential consequences, whether they are good or bad.

Chapter Summary

Not all financial risks can be eliminated.

Where do you stand on the financial risk-taking meter?

Do you avoid the risks, transfer the risks, accept the full risks, or try to mitigate them?

Know that your comfort with a financial risk can change over time.

Make sure you fully understand the risks that you are taking. A calculated risk implies that you have quantified it, otherwise it should be simply classified as a known risk. The results of taking risks that have not been measured can be a potential bumpy or disastrous financial ride.

FINAL THOUGHTS - NO ABSOLUTE PROFITS AND DISRUPTIVE FORCES

I started this book by sharing how I began my out of town rental property journey. I have thoroughly enjoyed the journey that started over ten years ago. The experience and knowledge gained along the way has been incredible. I have captured much of it in this book. However, there are some lessons that remain ephemeral, but have improved my real estate portfolio on all metrics. Most importantly, I have grown as a real estate investor one thousand-fold.

I want to remind the reader of the reasons to consider becoming an out of town landlord.

- Geographical diversification
- Potentially better returns on your personal capital
- Real estate prices in your home base investment market have appreciated rapidly and are now over-priced
- Potentially better or faster price appreciation in other markets
- Typically lower purchase prices
- Less competition with other real estate investors
- Better affordability for renters

Important take-aways

Use the great geographical tools available on the Internet to increase your knowledge of out of town real estate markets.

Hiring a qualified and licensed attorney could be worth the cost.

Self-managing out of town rental properties can be difficult.

Having a responsible tenant may allow you to contract with them within the lease agreement for certain services.

Maintaining good relationships with your out of town neighbors has many benefits, including providing an additional set of eyes on your property, and public relations to fight against negative perceptions of you being an out of town landlord.

It is important to carefully consider the types of rental properties in which you want to invest.

Computing certain quantitative and qualitative analysis is imperative to success.

The real estate investor needs to determine how many out of town markets to invest in.

Getting the place rented is all in the packaging.

It is not wise to behave like Pearl the Landlady when interacting with your tenants.

A wise and good landlord keeps their commitments to their tenants by fixing things promptly when they break.

All of the above action items create "goodwill chips" which can be deposited in the landlord "goodwill chips jar" with the tenant, and you never know when you are going to need to use one of those chips.

Don't leave your home base without my checklist.

You should seek the opinion of a qualified tax professional before declaring yourself a real estate professional for tax purposes.

Financial risk-taking is totally personal, the factors involved are not static, and you need to truly understand the factors that will determine whether you can make a profit on your investment or not. If you do not fully understand the risk, or they are not completely calculated, then you may be taking an unnecessary risk, or a risk for which the financial impact has not been quantified.

What follows are some final musings that I think are relevant to real estate investing in both out of town and the home base market.

Opportunity costs and positive investment returns

It is imperative to remember in addition to the oversupply of real estate, it was the lack of profitable and positively cash flowing opportunities in my home market that had caused me to keep my powder dry there. I strongly believe that investment prudence comes not only from adhering to the fundamental principles of investing and specifically real estate investing, but also from vigorous independent thinking.

My inclusion of the Single-Family REITs ties right into that point. There are many real estate professionals who would never have predicted in a million years the number of players that have been created and are now dedicated to that real estate space. I, on the other hand, kept wondering why not, which was only because I came to real estate investing with an open mind and let the numbers speak for themselves. Does a property positively cash flow from day one? Is it one of the best opportunities for my personal capital for the level of risk which I am comfortable at this time?

My academic training and experience have taught me to let the numbers guide me, and then to overlay the qualitative factors after the calculations. That way provides a much better opportunity to actually achieve a profit. We have to remember that initial calculations are merely estimates or projections. What actually happens can be totally different from those projections, and why it is vital to input the best possible assumptions into those projections.

Paradigms and absolute profits

People feel familiar with housing because we live in it, can feel it, and see it. This familiarity and easy of accessibility causes many to think that becoming a landlord is far simpler than it actually is. Furthermore, far too many investors hold false beliefs around real estate investing. I have heard such things as, "You always make money investing in real estate." I have also heard "You can only make money investing in two and three-unit buildings or larger." I want to impart that one always needs to review and analyze each and every investment opportunity on its own merits. There is no paradigm that produces absolute profits consistently. Once one exists, the highest profits are gone. That is a fundamental principle of economics and finance. Once such a pattern is well known, everyone will attempt to exploit it, until the excess profit is diminished and everyone experiences average or lower than average expected returns, or it evaporates.

I began this book highlighting the cost of opportunity. That is an ideal way to start the investigation of what you should put your hard-earned money into. Whether a particular investment is a better place to put your money compared with another, based upon similar risk characteristics and your investment timeframe, depends on the expected return on your investment results. One must also review the quantitative results and overlay the qualitative factors, as well. Throughout various timeframes, the results of an analysis of a comparison between the same two investments may change. That is why it is imperative that one not hold onto any absolute profit beliefs about one investment over another.

Real estate investing, like other investments, is subject to economic cycles on a macroeconomic level. The economic cycles impact rental property prices, interest rates on mortgage loans, and rent levels. In addition, on a micro-level, real estate investing is influenced by the type of investment property, its particular location, and the property management skills of the people in charge of daily oversight, to name just a few factors.

Tax reform for mom and pop real estate investors

I believe that it is long overdue for much of the tax legislations passed in the Tax Reform Act of 1986 to be updated for the benefit of mom and pop investors. As a good example of my point, the $100,000 MAGI salary limit for loss deductions enacted is now equivalent to $257,508.28 on an inflation-adjusted basis. At minimum, the mom and pop investor would receive much relief if the dollar amounts cited were adjusted by bringing them up-to-date on an inflation-adjusted basis and then have them indexed to inflation.

I have a great reason for proposing the change. Doing so could help with the affordable rental housing issue. Landlords who are able to receive more loss deductions on their tax return might be more willing to accept lower rents. This is a different way to pursue the same goal as the Low Income Housing Tax Credits (LIHTC) which is meant to provide a supply of affordable housing. The LIHTC database, created by HUD and available to the public since 1997, contains information on 46,554 projects and 3.05 million housing units placed in service between 1987 and 2016[13]. While the program has successfully created millions of units of affordable housing over the years, the number of people paying over thirty percent of their income toward housing has increased in many markets. According to the Joint Center for Housing Studies of Harvard, nearly half of American renters are home cost burdened[14]. It states, "A large and growing share of U.S. households cannot find housing they can afford."[15] Legislation that provides improved tax incentives for mom and pop real estate investors might allow them to offer lower rents which through competitive forces could help those at the lower income levels.

Fragmentation

One of the primary reasons that residential real estate has allowed mom and pop real estate investors profit opportunities is that there is fragmentation in most residential real estate markets. What do I mean by fragmentation? I define it as when there are many players in a market and the majority of them do not have the ability to substantially influence market prices, versus a few very large players or operators that can influence real estate market prices, etc. Most market participants do not have the best or most complete information on market prices which could provide them with an advantage in the market and lead to profits or outsized profit opportunities.

---

13 Office of Policy Development and Research *U.S. Department of Housing and Urban Development website* dated June 6, 2018.

14 *Joint Center for Housing Studies of Harvard University website* under the Research and Affordability sections released in conjunction with their 2017 America's Rental Housing report.

15 Ibid website under the Research and Affordability sections

In such fragmented real estate markets, a few participants may gain better information or some other advantage over the other participants. That advantage could be such things as where to find the lowest priced materials or labor for rehabilitation of a property as a home flipper. Whatever the acquired advantage, they will exploit it and make higher profits than other market participants.

The residential real estate market had traditionally been the province of mom and pop investors. However, the abundant supply of homes during the Great Recession sparked the interest of private equity firms and apartment REIT operators to create Single-Family Home REITs as an investment vehicle to purchase those homes. As I mentioned earlier in the book, many observers initially thought this would be a short-term dalliance. However, they are here to stay.

What impact will they have on future residential real estate markets? First, it brings professionalism to this end of the real estate market. People with Chartered Financial Analyst designations (CFAs), and Master degrees in Business Administration (MBAs), Finance or Real Estate will be pouring over various hard data to determine the residential purchase prices and the rent levels. Those MBAs and CFAs will approach the residential market with business acumen by using quantitative and qualitative analyses to make real estate investment acquisition and disposition decisions. They have to provide constant reporting to management and the REITs investors, which drives the analysis and reporting work. Their highly honed analytical skills will provide them with the tools to pick the least efficient markets in which to operate. They will have the ability to have huge impacts on setting prices in those real estate markets, since they can have longer investment horizons which are not ended by the investor's death, as is usually the case with mom and pop operations. They also have lots of capital to invest in maintenance and upgrading properties. They will increase the amount of investment needed to offer the current market trends of amenities potential renters' desire in properties. Mom and pop investors will be forced to follow their lead in order to receive similar rents, or they will be limited to the less desirable renters in those same real estate markets.

They may also be forced to abandon certain real estate market trends if they do not keep up with the REIT competitor's level of maintenance and upgrades.

Furthermore, Single-Family REITs could bail in droves if the profit margins stop meeting their requirements or if they find that ownership of single-family homes are too inefficient. That movement would cause an oversupply of real estate to hit the local markets where they own property. The oversupply would hammer those markets with seriously depressed real estate prices for years. That might return certain real estate markets to the same conditions as they were before the Single-Family REITS arrived on the scene, or to even worse market conditions.

Disruption

The Single-family Home REITs are not the only disrupter in the real estate market. Crowd Funding will continue to have a major impact on other sectors such as multi-family housing, hotels, and commercial properties. The ability of small operators to access larger sums of capital will bring more competitors into these sectors. If a sufficient number of these Crowd Funded real estate operators enter certain markets, they may create an oversupply of rental property offerings or simply lower rents to get their properties filled. Those types of competitive pressures will ultimately squeeze rent margins for all market participants.

I hope that the reader of this book finds many of the things that I have shared useful. I have shared the good and the bad. I have been honest and fair while sharing real stories. I brought my pragmatic prospective, along with my knowledge and experience. My hope is that the information presented here has expanded the reader's knowledge and assists them in being a more successful real estate investor. And I hope that I challenged some preconceived ideas about the best investments and the best way to be a real estate investor.

APPENDIX

SOME OF MY FAVORITE REAL ESTATE BOOKS

Bergsman, Steve. Maverick Real Estate Financing: The Art of Raising Capital and Owning Properties Like Ross, Sanders and Carey. Hoboken, NJ: John Wiley & Sons, Inc. 2006

Garrigan, Richard T., John F. C. Parsons. Real Estate Investment Trusts: Structure, Analysis and Strategy. New York, NY: McGraw-Hill 1998

Keller, Gary. The Millionaire real estate investor. New York, NY: McGraw-Hill 2005

Loftis, Esq., Larry B. Investing in Duplexes, Triplexes and Quads; The Easiest and Safest Way to Real Estate Wealth. Chicago, IL: Kaplan 2006

Loftis, Esq., Larry B. Profit by Investing in Real Estate Tax liens. Chicago, IL: Kaplan 2009

Lindahl, David. Multi-family Millions: How Anyone Can Reposition Apartments for Big Profit. Hoboken, NJ: John Wiley & Sons 2008

Martinez, Matthew A. Investing in Apartment Buildings. New York, NY: McGraw-Hill 2009

Moskowitz, Joel S. The 16% solution: How to Get High Interest Rates in a Low-Interest World with Tax Lien Certificates. Kansas City. Mo: Andrews McMeel Publishing, LLC 2009

Prandi, MPM, Melissa. The Unofficial Guide to Managing Rental Property. Hoboken, NJ: Wiley Publishing 2005

Reed, John T. Best Practices for the Intelligent Real estate Investor. Alamo, CA: John T. Reed 2009

Reed, John T. How to Manage Residential Property for Maximum Cash Flow and Resale Value. Alamo, CA: John T. Reed 2010

Reed, John T. How to Buy Real Estes for At Least 20% Below Market Value. Alamo, CA: John T. Reed 2005

Reed, John T. Aggressive Tax Avoidance for Real Estates Investors. Alamo, CA: John T. Reed 1998

Robinson, Leigh. LandLording. El Cerrito, CA: Express, 2006

Taylor, Jeffrey. The landlord's Survival Guide for the new and Part-time real estate investor. Chicago, lL: Kaplan 2006

Vollucci, Eugene, E. How to Buy And Sell Apartment Buildings. Hoboken, NJ: John Wiley & Sons 1993

A FEW PICTURES OF MY OUT OF TOWN INVESTMENTS

2018 REAL ESTATE ACTIVITIES

Date   Hours

January 18   7.33
Craigslist Advertisement for Fayetteville, NC
Craigslist Advertisement for Bradenburg, KY
Craigslist Advertisement for Killeen, TX
Craigslist Advertisement for Atlanta, GA
Responded to prospective tenant regarding amenities and move-in costs for Piping Rock Road
Sent Fayetteville property manager email message regarding prospective tenant from Criagslist that had contacted me. Also, mentioned that we may need to lower the rent if we did not have a tenant soon
Sent property manager inquiry regarding prospective tenants for Unit A. Property manager mentioned that a prospect had completed an application

January 19   1.20
Communicated with prospective tenants regarding availability of T Drive

January 21   5.5
Wrote letter to tenant in South Windsor, CT regarding returning check-in list, Association rules and things on deck.
Wrote letter to condo board regarding noise complaint

Communicated with Killen, TX Realtor regarding acquiring a property in Copperas Cove

January 22   **5.4**
Sent email message to Piping Rock Road property manager regarding prospective tenants
Sent email message to Atlanta leasing agent regarding progress of prospective tenants
Sent Dugger property manager an email message regarding rental activity
Sent Fayetteville, NC property manager an email message regarding vacancies

January 23   **5.78**
2010 Real Estate Activities
Corresponded via email message with Atlanta leasing agent regarding progress of prospective tenants
Sent Fayetteville, NC property manager an email message regarding vacancies and requested condo pictures
Corresponded via email message with Piping Rock Road property manager regarding rental activity
Checked P.O. Box mailbox for rental property mail

January 27   **2.5**
Responded to Fayetteville property manager regarding the status of my payment for repairs.
Responded to Fayetteville property manager regarding prospect (husband and wife) that was approved and just waiting for security deposit

February 7   **.25**
Corresponded with Realtor regarding Jacksonville , FL property

February 8   **3.50**

Corresponded with Killeen property manager regarding finally having all 4 units rented

Corresponded with Realtor regarding Merritt Island, Florida property

Checked P.O. Box for rental property mail

February 9   **7.1**

Reviewed bank accounts for rent deposits

Researched , coordinated and scheduled for plumber to install toilet gasket

Picked up rent for West Street property

February 10   **7.75**

Corresponded with Brandenburg property manager regarding strategies for new tenant

Reviewed information sent by Killeen , TX Realtor for potential property purchase

Reviewed credit report of prospective tenant for Atlanta

Deposit rental checks at bank

Balance rental property bank accounts

Wrote and mailed checks for rental property bills

February 11   **1.25**

Reviewed application materials of prospective tenant and declined their application for Atlanta

February 12   **2.75**

Reviewed leases for Killeen

Corresponded with Fayetteville prospective tenant

February 13   **5.65**

Craigslist Advertisement for Fayetteville, NC

Craigslist Advertisement for Bradenburg, KY

Craigslist Advertisement for Atlanta, GA

Corresponded with Fayetteville property manager regarding vacancy
Discussed 2456 prospects with 2456 Laurel Circle leasing agent
Checked P.O. Box mailbox for rental property mail

February 14   **4.75**
Craigslist Advertisement for Fayetteville
Craigslist Advertisement for Bradenburg
 Craigslist Advertisement for Atlanta, GA
Sent prospective tenant additional information and pictures

ABOUT THE AUTHOR

Eric Judge works as a financial advisor and has over thirty years of experience in the financial services industry focused on investments, insurance, and retirement. He has worked for a number of Fortune 500 companies, including his current employer and such companies as Travelers and The Hartford. He also worked for a small regional brokerage firm, Advest, which was later purchased by Merrill Lynch. He has been an out of town real estate investor and landlord for over ten years. He is also an avid reader of financial publications.

Eric earned a Bachelor of Science degree and a Master of Business Administration degree both with a concentration in Finance from the University of Connecticut, as well as earning the CFP®, designation. The Certified Financial Planner Board of Standards, Inc., awards the CFP® certification to individuals who meet the board's requirements for professionalism in financial services. To gain certification, a financial advisor must pass the CFP® Certification Examination and the CFP Board's Fitness Standards for Candidates and Registrants, agree to abide by the Board's Code of Ethics and Professional Responsibility, and comply with the Financial Planning Practice Standards.

Eric volunteers for Junior Achievement and SIFMA in order to facilitate programs that provide financial literacy to young people in his local community.

Made in the USA
Middletown, DE
21 November 2019